"Ian has written a prophetica[...]
It is an invitation to the searc[...]

—John Ort[...]
Presbyterian Church; author of *Who Is This Man?*

"My friend Ian DiOrio hits the nail on the head in *Trivial Pursuits*. Significance in life isn't found through success, salary, status, or sex. It's the result of serving God by serving others."

—**Rick Warren**, senior pastor of Saddleback Church;
author of *The Purpose Driven Life*

"Thanks for this inaugural book, brother Ian! It promises to liberate many from the entanglements of our culture and many others from the chains of empty religion . . . it is a wonderful offer to join Jesus in finding our lives by giving them away and to laugh when folks try to convince us that happiness has a price tag."

—**Shane Claiborne**, activist and author

"Ian DiOrio, a thoughtful and insightful young leader, challenges us to be free from our natural compulsions. He winsomely invites us to become curators of beauty, grace, hope, and love. I am inspired by Ian to live in this artful way of love."

—**Dave Gibbons**, founder and lead pastor of NEWSONG;
founder of XEALOTS.ORG

"Ian DiOrio is a great communicator who does an amazing job of showing us what matters most. He dismantles many of the false hopes in our culture and points to Jesus, the ultimate source of hope for us all. Learn from this book and live its message, and you'll be filled with renewed purpose."

—**Jud Wilhite**, author of *Pursued*; senior pastor of
Central Christian Church

"Unhappy with life as you now know it? Tried all roads and found dead ends? Wondering if there is anything else? Or maybe you're wondering if the world is spinning out of control with no good end in sight? In *Trivial Pursuits*, Ian DiOrio is revealed as a competent and delightful guide to the place where numb hearts awaken, anxious minds relax, and despairing souls find peace."

—**Bishop Todd Hunter**, rector of Holy Trinity Church;
author of *Christianity Beyond Belief*
and *Our Favorite Sins*

"Life can often be confusing and disappointing. We sometimes take roads and later wonder why, and we can feel defeated and alone. What I love about this book is that Ian DiOrio is writing as one of us who has experienced these very things, yet comes through with great hope and meaning. But it isn't just a self-help, you-can-do-it type of shallow encouragement you will read here. Instead it is guidance that shows how we can align ourselves with God and the input and vantage point of life from God's Scriptures, which makes all the incredible, tremendous difference. But again, this isn't simple 'read a happy Bible verse and everything will be OK' advice. This is a true, 'living in reality with all its ups and downs' message of hope. If you are feeling that you are facing yet one more disappointment or wondering if you are putting yourself down a path that may end up empty in the end, you must read this book. It may give you the exact direction based on God's guidance to shift your thinking, which will in turn shift your entire life."

—**Dan Kimball**, author of *Adventures in Churchland:
Finding Jesus in the Mess of Organized Religion*

"Ian DiOrio, without question, is a modern-day prophet who seeks to adjust the contemporary nonsense of trivial fulfillment and success into a biblical worldview that quenches the thirsty soul, invigorates the postmodern mind, and incites the need for transformational action. The quotes from Kierke-gaard alone are worth the price of the book."

"In unpretentious and often humorous prose, Ian DiOrio draws our attention to the ways we avoid living real life. DiOrio does more than just rail against the prevailing culture; his own experience as a club DJ gives him a broad under-standing of—and sympathy with—the attractions of pop culture. Nevertheless, the stories DiOrio tells lead us toward a deeper reality and a deeper Christian life that is art more than just entertainment."

"Ian DiOrio's *Trivial Pursuits* is anything but trivial. It's a master tour guide through the amusement park that American culture has become. Bold, incisive, and beautifully clear, it forces upon us the questions that clear away the clutter so that we can once again live obedient lives to Jesus Christ."

"We live in a culture that threatens to lull us all into mindless-ness, and DiOrio's book helps us to see the subtle influences in our everyday lives that are dulling our hearts and minds. But he writes not just to join the critical voices; he writes to encourage us—especially those who care deeply about Christ's church—to be more purposefully engaged in our lives and in the redemption of the cosmos. The book would be an excellent tool for inciting weeks of discussions among disciples of Christ who want to live more mindfully when surrounded by technology and entertainment."

—**Dennis Okholm**, professor of Theology,
Azusa Pacific University

"God uses prophets to rip open the heavens in such a way that reality invades illusion. In *Trivial Pursuits*, former DJ Ian DiOrio anoints our eyes to see beyond the superficial to what is real and meaningful. As you read, you will come to realize that not only is the unexamined life not worth living, but the unexamined practices of the church lead to 'cultural capitulation' instead of transcendent beauty and a subversive spirituality."

—**JR Woodward**, national director of
the V3 Movement; author of *Creating
a Missional Culture*

TRIVIAL PURSUITS

Why Your Real Life Is More Than Media, Money, and the Pursuit of Happiness

Ian DiOrio

BakerBooks

a division of Baker Publishing Group
Grand Rapids, Michigan

Published by Baker Books
a division of Baker Publishing Group
P.O. Box 6287, Grand Rapids, MI 49516-6287
www.bakerbooks.com

Printed in the United States of America

Library of Congress Cataloging-in-Publication Data is on file at the Library of Congress, Washington, DC.

ISBN 978-0-8010-1585-4 (pbk.)

Unless otherwise indicated, Scripture quotations are from the Holy Bible, New International Version®. NIV®. Copyright © 1973, 1978, 1984, 2011 by Biblica, Inc.™ Used by permission of Zondervan. All rights reserved worldwide. www.zondervan.com

Scripture quotations labeled ESV are from The Holy Bible, English Standard Version® (ESV®), copyright © 2001 by Crossway, a publishing ministry of Good News Publishers. Used by permission. All rights reserved. ESV Text Edition: 2007

Scripture quotations labeled NLT are from the *Holy Bible*, New Living Translation, copyright © 1996, 2004, 2007 by Tyndale House Foundation. Used by permission of Tyndale House Publishers, Inc., Carol Stream, Illinois 60188. All rights reserved.

Published in association with literary agent Blair Jacobsen of D. C. Jacobsen & Associates, an Author Management Company, www.dcjacobsen.com.

14 15 16 17 18 19 20   7 6 5 4 3 2 1

To Julia, Semeia, Asha, and Zion DiOrio.

My dearest family, your presence and support
are daily signs that God is love.

I love each one of you.

Contents

Contents

Acknowledgments

Writing acknowledgments is like giving an acceptance speech for an Academy Award; you just know that you will leave someone important out. So in an attempt to give proper thanks to the many people who have made my life, ministry, work, and this book possible, I fear I will err on the side of length versus brevity.

Thanks to my dear friend Jared Herd for his unswerving support of me and my work. To my literary agents, Don and Blair Jacobsen, thanks for working so diligently to make this book possible. To my editor Jon Wilcox and the team at Baker Books, thank you for your enthusiasm and guidance. To friends Dan Olson, Karl Durran, Phylicia Norris, Derek Rishmawy, Aaron Flora, and my brother Joey Azterbaum, thanks for reading the first draft and offering helpful comments and suggestions. To my father-in-law, Dr. Joe Grana, for offering deep and reflective readings of my work, always with a scholar's sensitivity and a pastoral edge. Dad, thank you for being a force of so much good in the world and in my life. I love you dearly.

Thank you to the churches and leaders who have supported me as a staff member. To Dr. Jim Price and Mike Malatka, and the leadership of Diamond Canyon Christian Church, thanks for giving me a start in ministry and for modeling a church that fulfills the vision I describe in this book. Thanks to Todd Proctor and leaders of Rock Harbor Church for offering the pulpit to a twenty-five-year-old, wet-behind-the-ears preacher. To Rick Warren, David Chrzan, John Cassetto, and my dear friend Brad Baker, thanks for all of you who make Saddleback Church what it is. It has been an honor to partner with you over the years. The most enthusiastic and heartfelt thanks goes to Gene Appel and the leadership of Eastside Christian Church for their support of me personally and my work in all its forms. Gene, you are a shining example of what Jesus had in mind when he called people to follow him and lead the church. I am very grateful for your mentoring, friendship, and partnership in the gospel. To Jared Dunn, thank you for your friendship and leadership in my life. It is an honor to partner with you in so much. You are a dear friend, a faithful companion, and an inspiration in my life. And thanks to Mike Erre, senior pastor of EV Free Church in Fullerton, for marking my life in a significant way during our years together at Rock Harbor.

Thanks to Michael Jay Solomon and the board and leadership at Truli Media Group; it is such an honor to charge forward in changing Christian media together. To Jay Barbuto and Greg Arbues, and the entire board of the Center for Leadership at the Mihaylo College of Buisness and Economics at Cal State Fullerton, thank you for your inspirational leadership. It is an honor to serve alongside you.

To mentors known and unknown, thanks for your words and deeds: Stanley Hauerwas, Karl Barth, Dietrich Bonhoeffer, Saint Augustine, Saint Thomas Aquinas, Thomas Merton, Henri Nouwen, Cornel West, Martin Luther King Jr., Walter Brueggemann, N. T. Wright, Rick Warren, Timothy Keller, Henri De Lubac, Barbara Brown Taylor, Colin Brown, Richard Hays, Ray S. Anderson, Rick Roderick, Greg Boyd, Rick Beaton, Rob Bell, Todd Hunter, Don Thorsen, Gary Black Jr., Keith Matthews, Dallas Willard, Tony Baron, Steve Richardson, Gene Sonnenberg, John Derry, Paul Alexander, Curtis Holtzen, Roberto Sirvent, Jeff Swaney, Chuck

Milbauher, Willy Hernandez, John and Olive Drane, David Fitch, and many others too numerous to mention. Thank you! To all the unmentioned and yet loved friends and colleagues, thank you for shaping my life and thinking. Thanks to my family; my mother Leigh-Ann has been a rock of strength and support all of my life. I love you, Mom—dearly. To my dad, Raif, thank you for being an example and encouragement to me and our family. To my grandmother Val: you are the source of so much of what I am. Thank you for inspiring me and challenging me, and most of all, for believing in me since birth. To my grandfather Chet: you are deeply loved. To my brothers Joseph, Wade, and Jake: you are wonderful gifts. Brotherhood is a blessing beyond measure. Thanks to Sonja and Stephanie, who are the sisters in my life. To my in-laws (I despise the term), Joe and Linda Grana. You are both living examples of un-trivial lives. Thank you for your acceptance and love of me as your son. To my sisters- and brothers-in-law Jolynne and Joey and family, Joey and Gerard, and Keenan, thanks for making life special. To Danae: your place in our lives and family is such a gift. What you have given us is beyond anything we have been given. You are loved. To our family in the Lord, Jeremy and Andrea Gallegos: we are so grateful for you.

Last, but certainly not least, my wife, Julia. Julia, words are limited in describing the love, respect, care, and affection I have for you. You are cherished beyond measure. There is not a day that goes by that I do not honor God for the gift he has given me in you. Thank you for the countless hours of patience you have shown me as I prepared this book for publication. This would not, nor could have, happened without you. To my children, Semeia, Asha, and Zion: the joy of knowing you, loving you, and being your father is a gift beyond measure. Daddy loves you, believes in you, and is forever here for you. You and your mother are the special people who make my life rich and far from trivial. It is for this reason I dedicate this work to you. I love you!

Prelude

Why Doesn't Happiness Make Us Happy?

I'm an inquisitive person. Some in my relational sphere find this annoying, others endearing. Being inquisitive means I take advantage of the time I have with interesting people. I'm always armed with a list of questions that I pose to men and women of diverse ages, faith commitments, ethnicities, and social statures.

One question I frequently ask is, "If you had one wish for my life, based on your experience and knowledge, what would that wish be?"

Universally, I get the same response: "I wish you happiness."

I always smile to hide my confusion.

"Happiness? Why happiness?" I push.

I'm not opposed to happiness, but I often wonder why it is that, in our day, happiness has become our highest aspiration. Could it be because happiness oddly avoids definition? We have tasted it and touched it, but always seem to be a few feet away from fully knowing it. We want it and wish it for others, but have personalized it to such a degree that we are unable to articulate what it is our souls long for. We are jealous for the mystery of happiness. Hearing of others who dance with happiness, we wait patiently in the corner for our turn to take it for a spin.

For some, happiness means doing whatever makes you feel warm and alive in the moment, regardless of the cost. For others, happiness is experienced through hobbies and habits. The time between, say, surfing the perfect wave or drinking the most pristine wine is just so much litter on the ground. Many of us find happiness in the presence of those we love. Our spouses, children, friends, and family supply emergency rations of happiness when all other ventures let us down.

And for still others, happiness is a ghost that is always on the move, driving our ambitions and activities while our search for the elusive feeling continues. In midlife, many of us have a happiness checkup. Faced with our own mortality, we begin to evaluate commitments largely based on one question: "Does he or she or this make me happy?" If the answer is no, divorce papers are printed and signed, motorcycles are bought, and plastic surgeries are scheduled, all in an attempt to grab hold of happiness.

Happiness is uniquely personal and hard to define, and yet it is the goal of millions. It appears that in wanting happiness, we yearn for something that we don't fully understand yet believe we can't live without. All too often, if given the opportunity to achieve happiness at the expense of others, the end justifies the means and we leave a wake of sorrow behind us as we grasp a momentary surge of happiness.

Happiness is like a breeze on a blistering summer day. As we sit under the scorching sun, happiness momentarily blows a gust of relief upon us, hushing the heat for a moment. But after the invisible cool is gone, the sun, which never stopped burning, sets to sizzling our skin once again. We are often left with, in the words of Ecclesiastes 1:14, the useless habit of "chasing after the wind."

When others wish happiness into my life, I wonder whether or not they have resolved to be happy at any cost. To do so would mean violence upon violence in their relational spheres, so I doubt that is what is meant. I have, over time, come to understand their wish is not a wish at all, but a prayer. Even atheists pray for happiness. A prayer that hopes I discover fully what many have felt only partially. A prayer that my life may clasp hands with the fleeting figure of happiness.

I appreciate the thought but am still left uneasy by the notion that happiness will make me happy.

I want more than happiness, and I believe you want more than happiness. I am convinced that what you and I long for is not fleeting happiness, but a life of meaning, and meaning may come in the absence of happiness.

Some of the greatest acts of love ever to emerge from the human spirit were performed in the absence of what we would describe as happiness.

Jesus suffered and died to achieve joy, not happiness, and there is a massive difference between the two. Mother Teresa undertook poverty for mercy's sake, not happiness. Martin Luther King Jr. was martyred because he surrendered his life for a much greater purpose than happiness.

Countless numbers of people choose meaning over happiness because the cost of self-satisfaction is too high for those they love. Happiness can be meaningless, which is why I no longer trust it as some kind of end-goal. I refuse to surrender to a life that is devoid of meaning yet peppered with moments of happiness.

How about you? Has your search for happiness made you happy? Or has happiness tricked you time and time again? Have you been suckered by happiness?

I do not want to denigrate happiness, nor venerate depression. I simply wish to draw us out of our search for a momentary "feeling" and into a deeper question about the very purpose of our lives. My assumption is that you were meant for more than happiness. You were designed for purpose, joy, and meaning. My fear is that our true self and its divine purpose has been taken off course by the pursuit of happiness. This false pursuit of happiness has derailed the true north of the human spirit. God desires wholeness more than happiness.

I pray that through both famine and festivities you will come to discover that your thirst for happiness is in reality a silent prayer offered to God that petitions him to make meaning out of your life.

I pray you will be able to see through the many fancy idols of our time so you may live meaningfully in God as the true self you were created to be, even if it means reevaluating what you think makes you happy.

Introduction

When I was a young man, my church was a cathedral of fog machines and laser beams accompanied by the pulsating liturgy of electronic music. My church was the underground rave and club culture of Los Angeles. As a DJ in this nocturnal wonderland, I had the privilege of providing grooves that sent masses of partiers onto a spiritual journey of music, dance, pleasure, and laughter. For me, spirituality was what happened on the dance floor in some abandoned factory or seedy club, where people of all ages were propelled into sensory overload by a flurry of drugs and the steady, tribal-like drumbeat of house and trance music. From my early teens into my twenties, raves and clubs provided the landscape for every personal and spiritual journey I took.

Every year, I would travel wherever my music career would take me, from Los Angeles to San Francisco to Philadelphia and back again. For a good portion of my life I spread the gospel of electronic music to curious and seeking underground congregations from coast to coast. My career was particularly successful in the world of rave and club culture, which in the end is not saying that much. Nevertheless, it was a small fishpond in which I just happened to be a medium-sized guppy. I thought that I would eventually be a senior citizen DJ, wearing earplugs covered by headphones, never to leave the world that was my home and hiding place, but I was wrong.

———

I was raised in a very tolerant home that understood religion as a personal opinion, and thus it was not normally practiced in my family. My mother and my grandparents raised me for most of my young life without the help of my father, whom I met for the first time when I was twenty-nine. Consumed with making ends meet, my family saw religion as a hobby that we could not afford as part of our regular routine. Like many hardworking, spiritually progressive people, we perceived the four walls of the traditional church as holding prisoner that mystery we called God. It wasn't that my family was anti-church or anti-faith; it was just that religion was essentially irrelevant to the daily responsibilities and petty annoyances of life.

Growing up, I had deep and perplexing questions about the universe and my place in it. Encouraged to investigate and believe whatever I wanted to believe as long as I wasn't being made to believe it by some cult, I was supplied with a plethora of religious options found in books and magazines. *National Geographic* magazine, brimming with articles and pictures about ancient religions, stoked my religious curiosity. The only virtue that guided my spiritual quest was that I would have to think for myself and not fall into the murky trap of fundamentalism. So book after book, article after article, I surveyed as best I could the religious options. This freedom to chart my own course led only to more confusion and a growing sense of lostness. There were too many possibilities and too many traditions to choose from. How would I know which was right? The world was a confusing ocean of human longing and I was a small boat being tossed about, desperately searching for an anchor—one that would not come until many years later.

Eventually, I gravitated to turntables, spending much of my youth producing electronic music, throwing underground rave parties called "massives" for thousands of people, and DJing in some of the most prestigious underground venues. Music and club culture became my sanctuary. But when I was in my early twenties, and the buzz of my DJ lifestyle began to wear off, the same questions that had haunted my young teenage imagination returned.

What is my purpose in life?

Is there a God? If so, who is he, she, or it?

It was through a long and interesting train of events that I found myself reciting poetry and playing house music at what would turn out to be a church-sponsored open mic night where people were invited to share their art. Not being a Christian myself, I recited some poetry that was, to say the least, explicit. Welcomed with cheers and open arms for my unfiltered artistic honesty, I was invited to share my poetry readings and music at an actual church service. This was the first time I saw Christian faith in action.

"Really? Are you sure?" must have been my initial response to the young pastor who asked me to come. Fearful of saying no—I mean, if God was real I didn't want to start off our relationship on the wrong foot by flaking on our first date—I agreed to come.

I have to be honest. I was a little freaked out by the church. It was made up of people who were incredibly nice—in a very Ned Flanders sort of way—and who just happened to be fascinated by me and my story.

"You're a DJ?"

"What is that like?"

"Are raves as crazy as people say they are?"

What was ordinary to me was a topic of sizzling conversation for the Christians I encountered.

The irony was that they were interested in the life I was trying to leave behind, while I was deeply intrigued by the life that they professed to live. I was searching for God, not merely a place to share my expertise on the world of popular club culture. With good intentions and a healthy dose of curiosity, those kind and genuine followers of Jesus embodied a simplicity, a naiveté if you will, that I didn't want to corrupt with tell-all stories of underground culture.

I came to realize that their interest was more about the intersection of God and my strange life. How does a person go from mixing turntables to wanting to spend time presenting his art to churchgoers? I understood that their curiosity resembled my own. All of us were on a search for God. Some were born within the walls of the church, which supplied them with categories and moral codes that encapsulated the divine. God was, to me, a blurry image, merely pixels and color, which gradually became more clear the closer I got to him.

I learned that the church, a strange and fragile institution with an intriguing and complicated past of its own, reflected in worship and work a pristine image of the One whom my heart and soul had searched after and longed for. If the church said God was who they had to offer me, then the church is where I would go.

I spent about a year in traditional church, going to different services and Bible studies. I felt very awkward at first, like I was an undercover sugar junkie at a weekly health club meeting. Everyone I met seemed so "together" and pristine. I was a hot mess. They spoke of God as a living reality in their lives, whereas for me he was merely an idea that I was working out in my mind. Eventually, though, God moved from being an idea that I thought about to the source and goal of my life. In March 2001, I came to faith in Jesus as the foundation of all my hope and meaning, and he and his kingdom became the purpose of the rest of my existence.

Jesus Christ, along with the deep and beautiful faith that bears his name, offered me an endless well of living water to drink from as God restored energy, vision, and passion to my life. I immersed myself in the rich and complex world of the Bible and the theological traditions of the church. My conversations went from the trivial to the substantial as I waded deep into a new reality of faith, worship, and study. Over time, I was asked to serve in various ministries, which eventually led to a deep and abiding sense that God was calling me to be a pastor, even though I had no idea what this meant or would ultimately entail.

Church as a Club?

Early on in my faith journey, a group of well-wishing young pastors invited me to a large pastors' conference that was focused on revitalizing the church. With only a few months' experience in church life under my belt, I had no desire to revitalize anything. Survival was my goal. Yet I went to the conference, seeing it as another opportunity to grow in my newly acquired faith and calling to be a pastor.

We arrived at the arena where the conference was being held, and as we approached the lobby, we were greeted with a very familiar sound: loud and bumping dance music. As we entered the main room where teaching and worship would take place, a DJ was in the corner playing old (at least to me) electronic hits. On the center stage were club kids, a peculiar tribe found in rave and club culture who wear outrageous gender-bending outfits coupled with huge-heeled shoes, making them look extraordinarily tall. Each attendee received glow sticks as they walked into the fog-filled auditorium. I honestly thought someone had called the event planners and told them I was coming in an attempt to pull a big gag on me. But, of course, that wasn't the case. It was an attempt at cultural relevance, I suppose.

Surprised at this attempt to clone the underground rave customs that had formed my first spiritual home, I took a sweeping look at the spectacle and turned around, swiftly walking back out to the lobby. At the time, I didn't know exactly what motivated my exit other than a feeling of longing and sadness. Upon greater reflection, I was shaken by the fear that there was no place, no people, who were living a life based on actual events, even Christian leaders. Raves, for me, were plastic, artificial, pharmaceutically driven, and temporary. I was longing for, and still do, the tangible, real, pure, and eternal. My pastor friends followed me out and immediately started asking questions.

"What's wrong, Ian?"

"You're a DJ. You love this stuff. What's the deal?"

"The church is changing to the rhythm of the world that we live in. What's your dilemma?" Or something like that.

My well-intentioned friends seemed to assume that in my newly discovered faith, I was looking for a replication of my previous years with a little Jesus sprinkled on top. I was sick of and exhausted by the superficial existence that had made up most of my days. I had been entertained to a point of numbness and was looking for something palpable and unique, not merely a "churched" nightclub. I wanted substance. I was emaciated by endless and empty weekends of malnourished diversion. I wanted God to strengthen my bones, restoring vigor to my spiritual body. I wanted a church to eat with, not be entertained by.

What I found instead was a group of faithful, loving, and dedicated people who were interested in me and my cultural past because they were apparently bored and fed up with their current church experiences. This was an odd revelation for me, as you can imagine. Needless to say, I was confused. I wanted to sprint away as quickly as I could from the petty world of my past into a new world where questions of human meaning were primary and the trivial distractions of life were secondary. I longed for real community, coupled with real love and sorrow, joy and pain, grounded in profound questions and deep, soul-searching answers. I wanted a life based on actual events, not culturally copied performances.

Fame, money, status, and the endless need to be current were what I had hoped to escape. I wanted to renounce my citizenship in the land I was raised in and become naturalized into a new, totally *other* way of life as a citizen of heaven.

━━ ━━ ━

What I have found, time and again, is that a force has captured the imaginations of Christian leaders and disciples that subversively trades the richness and otherworldliness of the gospel for a small and thin portrayal of God and his actions in the world. Christians possess a gifted power that is sadly dormant in millions of disciples' lives. It is this power that drew me into the strange world of the Bible and its players, yet many believers have lost the plot.

The church has become my true home, yet in small and sometimes unnoticeable ways it has been hijacked by a force that demeans God's majesty and devalues his children's true identity and the church's divinely sanctioned calling. What force am I referring to? The trivial and mundane cultural products that have the power to detach us from real life, abandoning us to a routine and numb existence.

Trading Champagne for Swamp Water

The trivial happens everywhere. On crowded street corners where human zombies wait for the crosswalk to blink with permission. Over radio waves beamed into cars zooming from here to there, swimming through concrete oceans littered with human traffic. In countless hours of surfing the web yet never catching any waves of inspiration or meaning. On every magazine cover, every gossip column, and all successful TV shows. It's in most of our transactions, sucking money away as quickly as a vacuum does lint, shaping and forming us into its image and likeness. It is never far from us; in fact, many aspire to be carbon copies of cultural fads and sadly most never escape from becoming so. The trivial captures our imaginations and values, our hopes and dreams, our heroes and villains, and leaves the souls of men and women created in God's image as nothing more than human holograms. These forces overwhelm and shape much of our lives.

The trivial is made up of the endless and void expressions of life that become the bankrupt sources in which people are searching for—but never find—meaning. The trivial is found in the world of tabloid magazines and reality TV stars, and the hope that money has the power to buy one's identity. The trivial is what has traditionally been least important in societies, yet somehow has become what dreams are made of in our current cultural context.

The word *trivial* is derived from the Latin word *trivium*, which literally means "place where three roads meet." Though it sounds complex, as most Latin terms do, it really is quite simple. *Trivial* refers to what can be found everywhere and is commonplace. There is nothing of depth or real beauty in the trivial.

The related word *trivia* refers to endless and almost always inconsequential tidbits of information. *Knowledge*, on the other hand, is the essential pillar of any moral and functioning society. In Judaism discernment and knowledge are essential parts of negotiating who you are and who God is. "The heart of the discerning acquires knowledge, for the ears of the wise seek it out."[1]

In Old Testament accounts, substance and depth were the byproduct of knowing God and living in the realm of his love. The repeated prohibitions against idols in the Hebrew Scriptures are not incidental words of caution to the Jewish people; they are a full frontal assault against holding up the commonplace as worthy of worship. A chunk of clay or bronze formed into an image of an animal or a mythical god never deserves worship or loyalty because it is the product of human imagination and creativity. The longer these acts of idolatry continue, the more the trivial becomes a false ideal. God desires not to prudishly restrict the lives of his people by his prohibitions against idols, but rather to liberate us from being just like the surrounding culture that does not know the true God of the universe. God's people are to have a witness in the world that shines brightly among the commonplace culture.

But something has happened. There has been a cultural shift. The tectonic plates of culture have silently slipped into oblivion right under our feet. The result has been an earthquake shaking the human spirit into fragments resembling raunchy film trailers and YouTube clips. Millions have dethroned beauty, the investigative hope that fuels the human spirit, settling instead to be spectators of pixilated fantasies and participators in endless transactions all affirmed as canonical truths, deepening the void of meaninglessness in and among us. Many of us have sadly settled for drinking swamp water rather than champagne and using neon lights to shine the way to freedom instead of the blazing, eye-twitching glory of the sun.

Who knew that, in our time, nihilism would look more like *Jersey Shore* than Friedrich Nietzsche?

So what is at stake if we build our lives on the temporal, passing fads of our time? I fear more than we realize.

Not only are our lives cheapened, but God, whom we love and represent to the world, is tarnished when, for instance, his people can quote Snooki more readily than Jesus. The shallowness we are soaked in is a soul-shaping illusion that prevents people from moving toward the depths of reality and truth that God offers. We live in a day of junk food and junk thought. We make image into an idol, and our endless praise of human fiction causes us to lose out on our true identity.

Over the years, I have been a leader, communicator, and teacher to thousands of people, many of whom are college students and young adults. I have witnessed time and again these precious and wonderful people giving their lives away to lesser goals and even lesser gods. Countless people of all ages are consumed by pursuits that demean and rob them of all

God intended. Whether it is chasing a media-driven fantasy, the illusion that money and fame will ultimately satisfy, or the proverbial fountain of youth gained by nips and tucks, people made in the image of God daily lose out on real and exquisite expressions of life because they are consumed by an illusion.

When illusion has become more real to us than reality, what should we do? I hope to unveil the power of the damaging illusions of our time, such as our fascination with media and entertainment and the endless pursuit of youth and wealth. These pursuits are akin to chasing after the wind and nothing more. But there is a way out of the fog into a glorious and abundant reality that has been neglected by many, if not completely forgotten. The hero with the power to liberate all of us from an inferior and counterfeit life is as ancient as he is current. Our hero and our hope are found in the God who was and is and is to come, and his beloved bride the church, who is the only hope for substance in a world of trivial pursuits.

Part 1

THE PURSUIT OF HAPPINESS

1

The Self under Siege

The 2008 Pixar production *WALL-E* is not merely another summer fun family feature; rather, it is a social commentary painted on screens across the world about the future of the human race and the predictable epidemic of a consumerist culture of carelessness. Shrouded in stunning computer animation, the real power of *WALL-E* is not in its flickering pixels but in its message and criticism of our time.

WALL-E is set in a postapocalyptic world in the year 2805. The serene and picturesque beauty of planet Earth, with its light blue seas and its horizons, along with its deep green and robust brown lands, has been leveled by seven hundred years of mass consumerism facilitated by the megacorporation Buy-n-Large (BnL). Earth is now an abandoned planet covered in trash, filth, and death. Giving up on restoring the hemorrhaging ecosystem, BnL instead evacuated Earth's population in fully automated and luxury Starliners, leaving behind an army of trash compactor robots called "WALL-Es" to clean up the mess.

After five years, however, the planet is deemed too toxic to sustain life, forcing humanity to remain in space. The world that was home to every birth and funeral, every first kiss and broken heart, is now a vacant desert of decomposing junk and refuse. Humans have become displaced by their own choices. They are, in the end, refugees of their own will.

Avoiding the painful reality of what they had created and their innate moral responsibility, these humans live in an insular environment far away from the decomposing planet they left behind, an artificial world of luxury and entertainment. Starliners, unlike the perilous planet Earth, are the ultimate and endless vacation, a cruise through the cosmos instead of the Caribbean. Life for humans is a living and breathing La-Z-Boy recliner (quite literally). Sitting in the mobile comfort of an automated recliner, stocked with all the technological resources they could need or desire, these humans are dreadfully obese and intellectually comatose. Their lives, if you would dare to grace them with such an honorable description, have become a Ferris wheel of hedonistic and mind-numbing activity, devoid of any purpose or meaning. Their mass consumption on Earth has, in the end, consumed their very humanity and forced them into space as fragmented and apathetic human shadows. All they know now is a sophisticated illusion, fashioned for the purpose of keeping their endorphins pumping and their brain waves static. Their demise began on Earth through what appear to be small but serious choices of disengagement. Pleasure compounded upon pleasure, dissolving every shred of temperance and restraint known to the dignity innate in humankind.

The message of *WALL-E* stings a bit. It is a digital mirror placed in front of our faces. It is a film that speaks of loss, but a type of loss that is subversive and hushed in a globe of noise and shadow. The loss that *WALL-E* points to is the loss of our essential humanity. It is the loss of the perplexing joy of self-discovery. It is the loss of "knowing thyself." Because in the end, the people of *WALL-E*'s world will trade personal knowledge, much of which comes at the expense of painful trial and error, for the ever-constant injections of entertainment.

The message of *WALL-E* is about the *trivial*, and what happens when we become desensitized to the world and our place in it. The confusion of our place in the world leads to mass consumption in the hopes that some product will root us and give us meaning. When we eventually realize that no product or show has that much power, we fall into apathy.

Apathetic Angels

WALL-E paints an all-too-realistic picture of human nature's penchant to choose comfort over curiosity and pleasure over purpose. People, who were created a little "higher than the angels," can easily forget the profound poetry that made and purposed them, resigning themselves instead to endless pleasure-seeking.

Why? Such pleasures serve only one purpose: to entertain and amuse. This endless desire to be entertained and fulfilled through anything other than God and his unique place in our lives eventually strips us of the patience, passion, and power to become all that God intended us to be. We become detached from the world and ourselves, ultimately becoming passive spectators in a planet of titanic problems and needs. The wild world of entertainment was once a leisure activity, embarked upon after the day's jobs were done and the higher human priorities of time with God, family, and friends were finished. Unfortunately, entertainment has become an essential commodity indispensable to our society's story, selfhood, and economy.

A recent study on media in the lives of eight- to eighteen-year-olds gives statistical weight to a delicate predicament:

> Over the past five years, young people have increased the amount of time they spend consuming media by an hour and seventeen minutes daily (from six hours and twenty-one minutes to seven hours and thirty-eight minutes)—almost the amount of time most adults spend at work each day, except

that young people use media seven days a week instead of five. Moreover, given the amount of time they spend using more than one medium at a time, today's youth pack a total of 10 hours and 45 minutes worth of media content into those daily seven hours—an increase of almost two hours of media exposure per day over the past five years.[1]

This colossal amount of information overload comes at a profound emotional and psychological cost. The fancy word for that cost is *anhedonia*. It is the opposite of the more used and recognizable word *hedonism*, which refers to the unending pursuit of pleasure.

Anhedonia describes the inability to sustain pleasure. It sets in the human spirit when what you thought would make you fully happy—that new car or job, that vacation of a lifetime, or that special someone—is ultimately a letdown. Anhedonia echoes loudly in the famous quip of Oscar Wilde, "In this world there are only two tragedies. One is not getting what one wants, and the other is getting it."[2] Wilde was a famous hedonist who pursued pleasure with voracity. Yet upon reflection, when recalling how he had fulfilled all he desired, he realized that at the end of the rainbow was not a pot of gold but rather a bucket of disappointment.

Haven't you experienced this as well? I know I have. There have been many times in my journey where I thought I was centimeters away from fulfilling my desires. Yet time after time the happiness was temporary. What you expected to result from this action or product or person—an adventure, or a sliver of human meaning—actually turned out to be an experiential dud. Our short experience of pleasure is often disrupted when we see others with an upgraded version of the product (or, sadly, person) that we truly believed would be our final gateway to perennial pleasure.

So what is a primary cause of anhedonia in our culture today? You guessed it: entertainment. "Among the factors that have been identified is our society's orientation toward entertainment. We have become a nation of observers watching with increasing enthusiasm as the sensational show intensifies. Whether it's a reality show, primetime drama, or a presidential debate, if there is nothing sensational or extreme, then ratings plummet."[3]

When I was a child, my family would often have friends over to watch a heavyweight boxing match on Pay Per View. I still remember the fight between Mike Tyson and Evander Holyfield. What happened in the ring that night shocked the world. Tyson, who was losing to Holyfield, decided to play dirty and bit off a large portion of Holyfield's ear. No one in my home could believe what had just happened. Boxing, despite its inherent violence, was always thought of as a gentleman's sport with clearly defined rules and boundaries. What Tyson did was deemed immoral and outside the ethics of the sport. Boxing at this time was quite popular. However, these days a more violent and sensational form of televised fighting has dramatically surpassed the ratings of professional boxing matches—UFC and mixed martial arts, where rules are limited because fighting has now become "ultimate." The more violence the better. We want to see our modern-day gladiators bleed in HD for our entertainment. Anhedonia is active here. When we desire more violence and fewer restrictions, evidence of our inability to sustain interest and pleasure is made clear.

Another example that clearly demonstrates this truth is the infamous *Jerry Springer Show*. The syndicated "Trash TV" show is home to some of the most explicit and jaw-dropping moments on television. Frequent topics such as incest, adultery, zoophilia, pedophilia, pornography, prostitution, racism, strange and taboo fetishes, and gender-bending sex operations, are all on display intermixed with seemingly scripted brawls between guests. Because the show appears on daytime television, it bleeps out and shades over the profane and foul expressions of whatever human circus is on display. The restrictions of daytime television, however, merely create a deeper desire in the viewing audience to see beyond the censorship and view the fully exposed melodrama. This desire does not go unmet. How could it in a culture of unleashed entertainment?

During the show's most popular era in the late 1990s, the *Jerry Springer Show* released videotapes, and later DVDs, that were "Too Hot for TV." They contained the uncensored nudity, profanity, and violence that had been edited out from the broadcasts. These releases sold extraordinarily well and inspired similar sets from other racy television series. Eventually, the show started producing similar "uncensored" monthly Pay Per View shows and on-demand specials as well. People could not get enough of Jerry and his obscene guests with their outrageous stories and predictable outbursts.

One more significant example is the overwhelming use of pornography. False images of sex, the human body, and how it is supposed to perform when the lights are off have crushed the possibility for true intimacy among millions. Why? Because young people raised on this material have views of sex based on falsehood rather than actual events. Real sex and real connection is hindered or cheapened because a lie has settled into the mind as a truth, rendering true intimacy difficult—if not impossible.

Anhedonia is present when what once gave you pleasure—your favorite TV show, or pet project, or even relationship—becomes antiquated and boring. The spectacle that gave you intense gratification yesterday now merely provides a faint sensation of pleasure. You need more! So you buy another product, or find a different partner, or ramp up the level of thrill, and for a brief moment the rushing hit of joy comes. But after a while, even that feeling must be displaced by the new and buzzing experience of some greater pleasure. Eventually you find yourself numb to pleasure and pain, apathetic to a world filled with beauty and brokenness, magnificence and misery. When life becomes solely a journey into pleasure, apathy eventually sets in and our lives look more and more like the lives of those in Pixar's *WALL-E*. "We are people on the verge of amusing ourselves to death."[4]

Souls of Indifference

"I don't care." That was the attitude of Jonathan, a longtime faithful member of my church who left the faith his sophomore year of college. Jonathan was raised in the church, knew all the right answers to every Bible question, and even led a small group of high school seniors. But something happened to Jonathan during his college experience. He did not experiment with drugs or get a girl pregnant, he wasn't prone to cussing, nor was he drawn to doing crazy things on camera so he could become a YouTube celebrity. What happened was indifference set into his soul when it came to God and the meaning of life. He was simply disinterested in thinking about God and the big questions of life. He called himself a pragmatist and decided he would live life based on what he felt at the moment. His ultimate goal was happiness. When probed as to what that meant or looked like, he could not articulate an answer, only a vague reference to a feeling he had once in a while.

"Since God could never be totally figured out by any one person, why bother to expend any effort to truly know him?" he said. "The best we can do is enjoy the day and the simple pleasures within it."

Jonathan was not an atheist; he was merely indifferent, which is more alarming than atheism. If given the choice between apathy and atheism, I would prefer to engage in life and conversation with an atheist every time. Though we disagree on the most important point, we both agree that in life there are important issues that require a firm, thought-out stance. Jonathan was caught up in music and food and films, all wonderful things I may add, leaving little time or interest in investigating faith any longer. Church and God were found wanting and uninteresting. Sure, God existed, but he did not add much or require much, so why bother?

I wish I could say that Jonathan's situation is unique, but it isn't. Questions that have typically held societies together, giving them their anchor and meaning, are now met with indifference or even hostility.

What is the meaning in life?

Is there a God?

Is there life after death?

What does it mean to be good?

These questions and others like them have been replaced with tabloid fanaticism and pop-culture mythology. Substance has been replaced by spectacle. Whether it is the legal troubles of celebrity bad girls like Lindsay Lohan, or the wardrobe eccentricities of Lady Gaga, the sources of meaning for millions are found in the daily trials and tribulations of someone's life whom they've never met. This voyeuristic obsession disables us from peering into the depths of our own souls, because our eyes are turned toward the celebrity lifestyles of the rich and famous.

What are the results of this?

We become indifferent to timeless and soul-defining questions, resulting in apathy both in the life of the mind and in the life of social action. For instance, sociologist Robert Putnam observes,

> It is precisely those Americans most marked by this dependence on televised entertainment who were most likely to have dropped out of civic and social life—who spent less time with friends, were less involved in community organizations, and were less likely to participate in public affairs.[5]

The Nones

In light of this truth, it is not surprising that a large and growing group in America is that of the religiously indifferent. Heavily composed of young adults—those arguably most formed by entertainment culture—this group of people "neither care to practice religion or oppose it. They are simply not invested in religion either way; it really doesn't count for much."[6]

Of this ever-increasing group, some

may profess to be religious or at least to appreciate religion.
But the Indifferent are too distracted and invested in other
things in life and are sufficiently unconcerned with matters
of faith to pay any real attention to religion. Religion may
be fine, they are willing to talk politely about it if asked, but
religion is simply not a particular interest, priority, or commitment in their lives. . . . Indifferent emerging adults can
come from any religious tradition or from a nonreligious
background. Their motto, to put it in a nutshell, would be,
"it just doesn't matter that much."[7]

It would be a relief to discover that these religiously indifferent made up only a small piece of the spiritual pie.
But, in fact, the situation is otherwise. Of those willing to
articulate their religious stance, those who fall into the religiously indifferent category represent "at least 25 percent
of that population."[8] What this means is that one out of
every four people discards as meaningless those questions
that have driven human beings to their deepest insights and
to expressing their most awe-inspiring acts of charity and
love. One out of every four people emerging in America today
believes questions about heaven and hell, about God and the
Bible, about Jesus and his resurrection and life everlasting,
are irrelevant and unimportant in comparison to the latest
newsreel from TMZ.

And why do I care? Because I was one of them. I know
what it is like to settle for an immediate fix to calm my search
for meaning rather than the long, hard, and engaged road of
knowing oneself. As William Butler Yeats wrote years ago, "It
takes more courage to examine the dark corners of your own
soul than it does for a soldier to fight on a battlefield."[9] I fear
that among emerging generations there will be depreciating
interest in the virtue of such courage, and it is courage that
is the mobilizing virtue upon which the long journey of self-
discovery is undertaken. Be courageous!

I spent five years as a college pastor at a church adjacent to the largest state university in California. Every day I witnessed thousands of students zooming from one class to another with cell phones wedged tightly to their heads and glossed-over looks on their faces. Consumed with their daily school schedules, workloads, friends, and significant others, not to mention the uncertain job market that awaited them, these students walked like sheep without a shepherd through the confusing landscape of their college experience. Overwhelmed with all that comes with being a young adult, their relief was found in the promise given by the thousands of flyers plastered on car windows and storefronts advertising celebrity guest appearances at local nightclubs. It was not uncommon to witness students with great books of literature, religious studies, art, and science under one arm and a glossy half-page flyer offering a club night entitled "Real College Girls of Orange County with Celebrity Host Kim Kardashian" in their other hand. This is the kind of flyer that will often also advertise a "Slutty School Girl" competition, along with a special on two-dollar draft beers.

If there was ever a perfect picture of the tension we currently live in, this is surely it. We are stuck between two worlds, seeking either explicitly or implicitly for answers that seemingly lie just out of reach. In one hand resides the great and adventurous search for human meaning found in the history, literature, and traditions of the great religions, and in the other hand is a kitsch advertisement promising nights of hedonistic pleasure, facilitated by cheap drinks and reality TV starlets. And for at least a quarter of emerging adults, the quest for meaning does not make it beyond the pulsating dance floors and fog-machine illusions of club life and the entertainment culture. They have, in the words of the apostle Paul, "exchanged the truth about God for a lie, and worshiped and served created things rather than the Creator—who is forever praised. Amen."[10] When what matters most is exchanged for what matters least, humans become homeless in a world of fantasy, and culture is devastated by its addiction to an illusion.

Signs of Cultural Devastation

How would we know if our culture shifted in such a way that human meaning became secondary to entertainment and consumerism? What would be the signs of the times? Would there be any at all? If it is true that the "inability to conceive of its own devastation will tend to be the blind spot of any culture,"[11] how can we know for sure if we have been blinded by overexposure to the pseudo-world of media-driven fantasy?

Philosopher René Descartes famously wrote, "I think, therefore I am." By this he meant that he knew himself because he knew his thoughts, even his doubts, were absolutely his own. What if it is truer in our culture that "I am what others think, or make me think"? Could it be that we are immersed so deeply in a world of flickering fiction we are not aware that our very lives and desires are being scripted by mediums that do not just merely reflect our culture but shape it? What would be a sign, a hint, that we have regressed into the trivial and lost something that is essential to being made in the image of God?

I believe there would be at least three noticeable signs.

Narcissism

The first sign would be a subtle, if not deliberate, move into a culture of narcissism. Ironically, according to biblical tradition, human beings most lose their sense of self when they are solely focused on themselves. Death equals life and denial equals fulfillment, according to Jesus. The often-repeated mandates toward humility in Scripture reflect the clear realization that in this world of lakes and oceans and animals and forests, there exists a dimension of life that is always to be remembered and honored—the disproportionate relationship between humanity and God. The further away human beings move from this relationship, the more God begins to die in the human imagination, and people are left with the compulsion to make gods of themselves. The apostle Paul, when writing to his son in the faith, Timothy, warns him of this ensuing situation as a sign of the end of all days.

> But mark this: There will be terrible times in the last days. People will be *lovers of themselves*, lovers of money, boastful, proud, abusive, disobedient to their parents, ungrateful, unholy, without love, unforgiving, slanderous, without self-control, brutal, *not lovers of the good*, treacherous, rash, conceited, lovers of pleasure rather than lovers of God—having a form of godliness but denying its power.[12]

Now, before we start pulling out our Bible Code maps and calling up Harold Camping for his next end-times prophetic word, maybe we should think of the end times not only in terms of the events leading up to Jesus's second coming but also the time when human meaning and purpose come to an end.

It is because we have lost the very source of our importance that we long for it so and have propelled many among us to godlike roles known as celebrities. The worship of celebrities and the fascination with celebrity culture is a sure sign that we have exchanged the truth of God for a lie. Our culture longs for fame more than it longs for truth.

> We consume countless lies daily, false promises that if we spend more money, if we buy this brand or that product, if we vote for this candidate, we will be respected, envied, powerful, loved, and protected. The flamboyant lives of celebrities and the outrageous characters on television, movies, professional wrestling, and sensational talk shows are peddled to us, promising to fill up the emptiness in our own lives.[13]

Only a culture of narcissism attempts to fill its empty and devastated cup with the fragile and perishing lives of people just like us. Humans become displaced in the world and settle for triviality over abounding value when other humans are all we have to celebrate and worship.

Apathy

The second sign that our culture has regressed into the trivial and lost something pure and essential to its nature is the overwhelming apathy among people today. As we noted earlier, a massive and growing population is indifferent to big questions that have traditionally been the source from which human beings have drawn meaning. Apathy comes at the expense of feeling all we were intended to feel and all we were made to embody.

Christianity is a love-drunk, joy-filled faith that calls us into a quest that begins in imperfection and ends in glory. To avoid or withdraw from self-discovery, and settle for a silly and temporal marketing campaign instead, is to avoid oneself and God at one's peril.

Saint Augustine, one of Christianity's greatest minds and personalities, was in a sustained argument with other philosophers over the question of being apathetic toward life. Some of these thinkers proposed apathy as the only way to live, stating that the only thing one can do in a world such as ours is to live with quiet disregard for the pain and pleasure that is part of life. Augustine vehemently disagreed. To live life as God intended is to live open to the world as it is, which means passionate engagement with even the most imperfect. To not care about what matters most is to live according to the temperamental whims of your feelings, not God's will. That is why Augustine wrote, "But if by apathy a condition be meant in which no fear terrifies nor any pain annoys, we must in this life renounce such a state if we would live according to God's will."[14] If given the choice between escaping the real world in a flurry of manufactured indifference or confronting life as it is, no matter how difficult, confrontation is the only choice humans ought to make. This may indeed cause deep spiritual and mental conflict, but whoever said that beautiful lives are the product of frictionless ease?

Longing for Authenticity

Lastly, we can notice the devastation of a culture by not only what it produces but also what it longs for. Our longings as much as our loves instruct our search for truth.

What do you long for?

I suppose for many the constant and ever-expanding role of media and technology creates distance from the organic and material world of which we are a part, which in turn makes life feel a bit phony and plastic.

Authenticity is a buzzword used by ingenious marketers who appeal to our longing for something tangible. Authentic community and experiences are worth their weight in gold nowadays. This no doubt contributes, at least in part, to the organic revolution. Whether it is organically farmed coffee or free-range chickens, our culture yearns for untainted products and relationships. Large companies as well as house churches have adopted the "organic" lingo to justify their unique place in the world. Why is this so?

I would suggest it is because our very lives have been formed by artificial promises that have proven futile in bringing about true self-knowledge and joy. Plastic hasn't produced the pleasure we thought it would. The desire to know and be known, to move away from the fake machinery that makes our lives a walking and breathing wax museum, drives younger expressions of community and business, all under the guise of "organic." This longing for "reality," for true and authentic expressions of life, is a sign that our culture has been devastated by the onslaught of the superficial and the fake and is silently trying to rebel. Can you feel the rumbles of a famished culture?

Our longing for the authentic and the organic reveals much more about what we have lost than what we hope to gain. Could it be our longing for the organic is energized by our deep, internal sense that the world is off its hinges? The organic movement reveals that we want substance rather than shallowness; we want justice and harmony woven into the fabric of our purchasing power.

Where Do We Go from Here?

Where in our world and in our own lives have we replaced actual events for false ones? How can we detect if our real life has been subtly exchanged for a fake one? My attempts to explore these questions are humble gestures by one attempting to make his way through the maze we all live in. By the grace of God and through the power infused in the local church, I believe there is hope for real experiences and authentic forms of life that refuse to bend to the pressure of modern culture. Surely this is not a promise but a hope. Hope, we must always remember, is a grace and a virtue saturated with depth for those who worship the God of all hope.

We must not lose heart. The problems we face are significant and real, but our God is bigger and brighter than any computer-generated image or marketed product out there. It is my view that the local church will be the one place in the world that will have the power to offer a way of life transformational enough to redeem what has been lost and to send people out into the world with a renewed sense of power, passion, hope, and imagination. The church has the capacity to be the one place on the planet that shines as a beacon of hope in a dark and confused world.

The glory of the gospel is about "new creations," and God has not stopped renewing and restoring what has been tarnished and neglected. The gospel promises us a life that is rich and eternal. It is this life, and the God who offers it to us, that call us forward in hope and love. But before we arrive at the answer God would give us, we must first diagnose the symptoms of a sick and shallow culture if we are going to avoid succumbing to *WALL-E*'s world.

Questions for Reflection

Have you noticed yourself or others becoming slowly addicted to media and entertainment? What would be some signs of this?

What role does God play in shaping your understanding of the world? Or in other words, how does your view of God shape your daily decisions?

Would you agree that apathy and indifference are becoming more common? What signs do you see that reveal this truth?

How do you think you can combat apathy and spiritual indifference?

2

The Light of the World

As a child, I was terrified of the dark, which is ironic considering much of my life was spent in nightclubs. The cool, bleak nothingness that arrived with the flick of the light switch would consistently awaken my imagination to all of the monsters and bogeymen that lived under my bed and in my closet. Night after night, I would lie still in my bed, as rigid as a dry piece of spaghetti, attempting to settle my mind and overcome my fear. It never worked. Every night was an exercise in futility. Off to bed I would go, eventually to be overwhelmed by the creepy feeling that came with being alone in the dark. I soon learned to place my fear and anxiety in the safe and reliable care of the one and only "light of the world." No, it wasn't Jesus that saved me from spine-chilling night terrors. Rather, it was the only light of the world I knew at the time: my TV set.

In my small room resided a humongous television. Comprised of more wood than TV, this behemoth was the centerpiece of my little space. Whenever I was afraid of the still silence of the night, I would turn on my TV and the lights and sounds would lull me into slumber. It didn't matter what was on, whether *I Love Lucy* reruns or a cheeky infomercial; all that mattered was that it was on and its presence soothed and comforted me. Like a Technicolor babysitter, my television was a real and living presence in my room that drew me away from my childish fears and nightmares. As long as the TV was on, I was out of harm's way. As long as the TV was on, I was assured that night would pass gently into day.

I wish I could say that I outgrew this habit with age and maturity, but I didn't. Even today, my television is often on, still beaming rays of comfort to my subconscious.

It is a rare thing these days to go to a restaurant where there isn't a plasma TV on every wall, like distinguished art strategically placed in a highbrow museum. There, in the background of your dinner conversation over chips and salsa, television provides the noise and stimulation that fills the awkward empty spaces that occur in most friendly conversations.

"Oh look, the game is on."

"Really, who's winning?"

"The Cubs are up by one."

"Great! This could be their year."

"Not likely."

And then off to commercial.

Where I live, gas stations now have small televisions built into the gas pumps that are triggered when you start filling up your tank. Commercials, news, and scandal provide a backdrop for the mundane exercise of fueling up your car.

For some unclear reason, we have constructed our society so that media devices are everywhere. From small screens that fit in the palm of your hand to massive Jumbotrons such as the one in Times Square, visual media has become part of the natural landscape of our cities. And much of the time, they do so without being noticed at all. Why is this? Could it be that we have not outgrown the childlike dread of silence, seclusion, and being alone in the dark?

Certainly the way we construct our world tells us about the ideas that form our values and most vital views on life. The ten-dollar word for this is *ideology*. Ideology is not always clear. It has a way of living in the cracks of language and worldviews, being expressed in media, film, architecture, and food. Ideology may best be summed up by the phrase "They don't know it, but they're doing it." There is a hidden ideology present with the primacy and placement of media, but what is it? The answer isn't obvious. But there is something eerie in how our world is so dependent upon and fascinated by these screens and the stories they tell. Just ponder for a moment the amount of time the average American dedicates to watching television.

When evaluating leisurely activities of Americans in 2009, the United States Department of Labor concluded that "watching TV was the leisure activity that occupied the most time (2.8 hours per day), accounting for about half of leisure time, on average, for those age 15 and over."[1] Leisure activities such as talking with friends over coffee, playing sports in the park, going for a jog at sunset, or playing board games with your kids were all secondary to being docile before a TV. In just two years, the number of hours spent watching television increased at a jaw-dropping rate.

> A television is turned on for six hours and forty-seven minutes a day in the average household. The average American daily watches more than four hours of television. That amounts to twenty-eight hours a week, or two months of uninterrupted television-watching a year. That same person will have spent nine years in front of a television by the time he or she is sixty-five.[2]

Did I say jaw-dropping? Jaw-breaking may be more appropriate. Too often, the posture of human beings is one of passively sitting and watching. We have moved from being actors in life to spectators of portrayals of life. Our seemingly ordinary existence pales in comparison to the drama on-screen, so we use television as a means of escape. Because television has become a powerful shaper of culture, our interior life is increasingly formed by its influence. We truly believe that these images teach and train us in what it means to be current and fashionable and relevant. Our "real lives" are constantly being swept up in, judged, and formed by the syndicated fantasies that march their way into our world, many times without beckoning or permission.

We allow this invasion for familiar reasons. The televised world is better than the real world. In fact, to many of us, the televised world *is* the real world, the safe world. It is the world that helps us know about our own world. Without it, our world would feel as shriveled as a week-old banana peel. Whether it is the nightly news offered without "spin" or "slant," or the new episode in your favorite long-standing sitcom, television has a way of making us feel more connected and in tune with the outside world and therefore liberates us from the normalcy of our jobs and friends and responsibilities. "The pleasure obtained from a television . . . is experienced as 'real' freedom. No one experiences this as alienation."[3]

For instance, let's think about love. Do you measure love based on what you see in everyday life, or is love measured by the romanticized examples offered on television? In TV land, real love isn't the messy and quirky experience of sweaty palms and misplaced kisses. No, love is sexy, passionate, and perfectly scripted. Even love gone bad, as often found on hit shows like *The Bachelor* or *The Bachelorette*, is orchestrated with precision.

Or let's think about war. For most Americans, our only experience of war is mediated through television. It is a collection of clips and images, bereft of their most awful highlights. War, in TV land, is not a tangible, bloody, and horrific mess that would snap our comforts in half if we saw it up close; it is a one-minute newsflash, a brief synopsis that quickly moves into commercial.

Whether it aids our search for pleasure or our desire to escape pain, television has become more than an unexceptional appliance, such as a microwave or coffeemaker. It is an instrument of power—ideological power, to be exact. Wielding more persuasion than a savvy and well-scripted car salesman, television has the power to absorb our lives into its own reality and ultimately confuse in our minds what is real and what is counterfeit. The "light of the world" leaves our search for meaning darkened, and we are left to look to the triviality of other people's scripted stories to try and answer our own deepest questions. In our fascination with television, we are searching for a story that has the power to cement the fragmented pieces of our lives together. But the question remains whether television can give us what we so long for.

Searching for a Story

Whether it is a story about a hero and villain duking it out in the endless battle between good and evil, or two lovers ripped apart by war and family, stories are woven into the fabric of our world and inform much of our personal identity. Whether it is the religious scene and its stories about the origins and purpose of the world or political regimes and their stories of progress and utopia, stories in this context are often told to bewitch people into obedience, submission, alliance, and participation. Though we live in a world that supposedly has little time for metanarratives as such, it still seems that the universe spins and bows to a great story. Wars are fought and ceased, freedom is purchased and withdrawn, love is forged and forgotten, life is taken, death is defeated, all of life bends toward a great ending—stories triumph over all.

One could almost say that human existence is the search for one's own story. Each person, when they are born, is given a bare-bones script with a few characters intact. The dealings that take place in life are largely formational in who one becomes. Whether you are a hero or villain is your decision. And to some, the choice is a vocation that arises out of a series of events, all of which make up our personal tapestries of human life. The power that television can hold is that it offers a story in which to find yourself without having to go through the actual events, sometimes painful, that forge human character. You can discover who you are by watching others rather than wandering through the trials and beautiful peculiarities of life yourself. Captured by another's story, we often subconsciously search for our own story within it, finding only wispy shadows of life as represented by the commercials that interrupt what we watch.

For a moment, take for granted that nine years of your life will be spent watching television. Now imagine that you are at the end of your life. Your hair has turned gray and sparse, your skin has lost its firmness, and your sharp mind has grown dull. Only weeks away from leaving this life, you reflect on the way you spent your days. Memories are conjured up of finding your spouse and raising your children. Trophies and awards flash before your eyes, reminding you of all the great accomplishments and contributions you made to the world. And then you get a surprising mental image that startles you: you are sitting in front of a television. Nine years of your one and only life were spent staring at a screen displaying the stories of other people's lives. How do you feel about this? Are you satisfied with the way you lived your life? Would your search for a story be satisfied?

When described this way, most of us would stagger back and say, "Of course I'm not satisfied! I don't want to, even in part, be defined by the years I spent watching television." Yet since most of us do not give much thought to the dominant role of television in our lives, we are absorbed into its magnetic pull without thinking twice about the consequences.

So why is it that we spend countless hours glued to the tube? Why does the television hold such a significant and privileged position in our lives and culture? What motivates us to give so much time to stories and lives, both real and fictitious, that in the end have very little to do with our own?

TV Therapy

Imagine coming home after a long and laborious day at work or school and settling onto your comfortable couch to watch your most treasured sitcom. Picture your shoes coming off, your tie or belt buckle loosening, and your favorite can of soda popping open with that lovely and familiar hissing sound. Remember the wizard-like feeling that comes with gripping your remote control in one hand and pressing the "on" button. What show are you going to watch? Why? What about it draws you in, or, should I say, relieves you of the mundane and often frustrating aspects of normal life? On a scale from one to ten, how would you rate your mental activity during the duration of your viewing experience? Are you paying focused attention, or are you just there, watching with a dull, zombielike look on your face?

What is taking place in the moments you spend watching television is a form of therapy. When I use the word *therapy* I do not mean the type of treatment that comes with deep and guided introspection, ultimately leading to consolation and self-discovery. No, I mean the type of therapy that calms your mind and pacifies you like a baby with her binky.

"When we turn on the television, we rarely want to be challenged. We want to relax, unwind, be entertained."[4] Phrases like "vegging out" refer to the posture of those who watch TV as a form of therapeutic release.

A team of British researchers conducted a study entitled "Household Appliances and the Use of Time." In this study, they concluded that "television is the cheapest and least demanding way of averting boredom. Studies of television find that of all household activities, television requires the lowest level of concentration, alertness, challenge and skill."[5]

The power and attraction of television is in its undemanding, comforting, and therapeutic ability to alleviate the frustrations and boredom of everyday life.

Television's most enduring contribution to culture is the twenty-two minute solution. The twenty-two minutes between a sitcom's introduction of a problem and the tidy solution often do not correspond to lived experiences of detox, the DMV, or divorce court.[6]

Unlike the considerable and complicated problems that plague our everyday lives, troubles in TV land are easily fixable. In fact, "shows that depress, anger, or upset audiences are anathema to television. Networks avoid tragic or controversial themes because advertisers want shows that put viewers in the buying mood."[7] For television to work as good therapy, it mustn't unnerve you. In fact, it seeks to sedate you. We see the therapeutic power of television at its best through the bizarre phenomena of canned laughter.

Invented by Charles R. Douglas in the early 1950s, canned laughter is used "to enhance or substitute for live audience reaction on television."[8] The television takes on a leadership role by guiding you in the moments that are supposed to be funny and relieving. Rock star philosopher and cultural critic Slavoj Zizek writes the following when reflecting on canned laughter: "In the evening, I come home, too exhausted to engage in a meaningful activity, I just press the TV button and watch *Cheers*, *Friends*, or another series; even if I do not laugh, but simply stare at the screen, tired after a hard day's work, I nonetheless feel relieved after the show—it is as if the TV-screen was literally laughing [in] my place, instead of me."[9]

When we watch television, we desire consolation, predictability, and rest. In many ways, we desire an escape from reality itself. We do not even need to physically laugh to feel relieved. The television laughs for us, bending that line between reality and fiction once again.

Our unshakable fascination with media is surely grounded in our obsession with celebrity, and one of its most remarkable messages to us is that all of us can escape the humdrum and monotonous reality that makes up our life by becoming one of *them*. We end up being TV refugees because we are more engaged in the powerful land of illusion than we are in the grip of reality, even if that illusion is called reality TV.

Small Gods for Fifteen Minutes

Renowned twentieth-century pop artist Andy Warhol famously remarked, "In the future, everybody will be famous for fifteen minutes."[10] When Warhol uttered this statement, those around him were perplexed. What could it mean for everyone to be famous? Fame is reserved for the opulent, the talented, and the spectacular among us, not the average Joe making ends meet with minimum wage. How could *everybody* be famous at all, even if for only fifteen minutes? Though Warhol's observation may have been bewildering years ago, today it doesn't seem that far off.

Reality television and social media sites now offer anyone and everyone, irrespective of talent, an opportunity to become famous for no other reason than being famous. Fame and celebrity have become detached from any particular genius or skill and have instead become commodities that one can claim just for living on the *Jersey Shore* or by being a *Real Housewife of Orange County*.

Because our technological devices keep us tuned in to what is taking place "out there," many of us feel exhausted by even the idea of introspection. It is easier to watch and to copy the lives of others than to explore the deep and complicated wells of human desire and emotion within ourselves. We settle for a life obsessing about the lives of others and looking for ways to imitate what we believe to be more interesting than what our own life circumstances seem to promise. We become what we worship, and therefore it is not surprising that the forms of self-expression we see everywhere are not really that at all but rather forms of celebrity replication.

If our attention is constantly aimed elsewhere for stimulation, will we ever turn inward to investigate our soul in silence? If the answer is no, then we run the risk of losing our ability to "see" altogether.

MTV once aired a reality TV show called *I Want a Famous Face*.[11] The show chronicled the journey of young adults who were dissatisfied with their God-given beauty and underwent the process of intense plastic surgery to look like their idol of choice. Celebrities that participants chose included *Baywatch* starlet Pamela Anderson, pop artist and *American Idol* host Jennifer Lopez, teen pop phenomenon Britney Spears, *People* magazine's "Sexiest Man Alive" Brad Pitt, Latin recording artist Ricky Martin, and famed Spice Girl Victoria Beckham. Young men and women, barely old enough to vote or drink an alcoholic beverage, spent thousands of dollars to undergo tremendous pain to look like someone they had deemed beautiful.

In our culture, you can become famous by unnaturally sculpting your face to look like a famous person. If there has ever been a clear example of the ideological power of celebrity culture, surely this is it. *I Want a Famous Face* takes our belief in the power of TV and celebrity to its very extreme. Shows like this preach a gospel of narcissism and illusion, and many of us have unwittingly become converts. Some truly believe that all you need to do for admiration and fame is make a small sacrifice of flesh to the god of reality TV, and you too can become a small god for fifteen minutes.

Cultural theorists call this *deterritorialization*. Don't let this big word scare you. Break it down a bit, and you will see the word *territory* hidden in its parts, along with the prefix *de*, which means "anti" or "against." Deterritorialization implies that the more someone is caught up in the land of media, the less they are formed by and connected to the local expressions of life that they live day-to-day. "People's sense of the world is no longer shaped simply by ideas, traditions, and customs that have been important in their local communities."[12]

Identity used to be formed by doing life with friends, family, and others in regional or local communities. Not anymore.

Now we live in a global culture rooted in media and image. We have become increasingly influenced and formed by whatever is televised and marketed to us, and less interested in the stories found in our own lineage. I like the way author Gordon Lynch puts it: "As people become less dependent on their local communities and cultures, and more absorbed into electronically mediated communities, so the way in which they make sense of life is increasingly shaped through the media content that they consume."[13] Doesn't the *I Want a Famous Face* phenomenon show this to be true? Our notions of beauty, morality, truth, and love are formed by what absorbs most of our time—namely, TV. And in the case of most Americans, the television is what takes us and forms us into its image.

Whether it is television or streaming devices, the rapid advancement of new technologies and their subsequent widespread use means we must take stock of how we use media and how it informs our identity as humans made in the image of God. Whether it is our desire for comfort and tranquility or our obsession with fame and power, the power of media is undergirded by the belief that human identity can be purchased and secured. We believe that we can buy or shape our souls via our purchasing power. Until we confront this powerful myth, our lives won't be based on our reality.

Questions for Reflection

What gives YouTube and digital TV such power in our lives?

How many hours a week would you guess you spend "watching" some form of visual entertainment?

Why are we as a culture obsessed with the lives of celebrities?

Do you think celebrity obsession has positive or negative affects on the human spirit? Why?

Do you agree that people use TV as a form of therapy? What are some of the cultural factors that cause people to want to "veg out" daily?

3

I Bought My Soul on eBay

Adam Burtle, a twenty-year-old atheist, decided one day he would have a little fun. This University of Washington student and part-time car mechanic placed his eternal soul for sale on the popular website eBay. With a starting bid at five cents, offers came in from all over the globe, eventually reaching $4,200 before the listing was removed and he was suspended from the site. eBay has blocked similar auctions in the past, but said Burtle's soul sale slipped through the cracks of cyberspace.

"Please realize I make no warranties as to the condition of the soul," Adam wrote in his posting. "As of now, it is near mint condition, with only minor scratches. Due to difficulties involved with removing my soul, the winning bidder will either have to settle for a night of yummy Thai food and cool indie flicks, or wait until my natural death."[1]

Driven more by boredom than an attempt to re-create a modern version of Goethe's *Faust*, the famous tale of a desperate man who resorts to selling his soul to the devil, young Adam illustrates an interesting and disturbing truth about souls as they exist in the human imagination: they can be bought and sold on the market for a fair price.

In January 2005, a different yet just as conspicuous marketing attempt took place. A Nebraska college student, age twenty-one, auctioned off his forehead as a fleshy billboard to the highest bidder. Needing money for college and beer, this young man exploited his body for profit, offering his skin as a smooth surface to sell the products and gadgets of the company who would pay the most for this prime piece of personal real estate. The winning bid accrued the student over $37,000.[2]

"For that princely sum, the young man spent thirty days with a temporary tattoo on his forehead extolling the virtues of a snoring remedy."[3]

Those who would see the ad, of course, would have to be in eye-gazing proximity to the famously inscribed forehead, but the news and shock of the story would ensure that the $37,000 investment would turn a swift profit for the makers of "No Snooze," the company who purchased the forehead for advertisement space. When asked by reporters as to whether there was something unethical with selling his forehead to gain a quick buck, the human billboard himself was quoted as saying, "The way I see it I'm selling something I already own; after thirty days I get it back."[4]

Notice the language used by the walking, talking billboard. He refers to his body as something he "owns." His body is interpreted in terms of property ownership and thus is equated to a commodity that can be bought, leased, and sold for money. In this specific case his body was rented, like ad space in a newspaper, even if only for a brief thirty days.

In 2009 Lavonne Drummond, an unemployed mother of six, ran into some financial trouble and decided to take her economic troubles into her own hands, or more accurately, her womb. This Arkansas woman, pregnant with her seventh child, decided to put her child's naming rights up for sale on eBay. The opportunity to name her seventh child would be the privilege given to the highest bidder. The auction started at a mere $150.[5] Lavonne posted the auction on eBay in hopes that she would receive enough cash to buy a "trustworthy" car and to relieve her sister's burden of supporting her cash-strapped family. Drummond told media that she was offered $15,000 from an unknown bidder, yet eBay thwarted the purchase because of its policies against their website being used as a form of lottery.

Sandra West, a California socialite, died at the ripe age of thirty-seven. Knowing her days were coming to a swift close, West made an out-of-the-ordinary demand in her will.[6] She desired her corpse be placed to rest in her favorite nightgown behind the wheel of her light blue 1964 Ferrari, with the seat slanted comfortably. The heiress, widow of Texas oil millionaire Ike West, was a wealthy member of the Beverly Hills elite, and she left most of her three-million-dollar estate to her brother—provided he followed through with her wishes. The Ferrari was encased in concrete so no one would be tempted to dig it up and drive off with the car that was destined to be Sandra's final resting place.

What do these four stories have in common? All of them reveal, in their own way, the strange, perverse, and life-altering effects of money on the human spirit. We have commoditized our identities and are open to the suggestion that our souls can be satisfied by things, that we have ownership over our souls and can do whatever we please in our endless pursuit of pleasure and meaning. Everything and everyone has a price. Money and what we can buy with it changes who we are in a million different ways.

Do we think so little of our souls as to believe we can put them up for sale? Do we put so little stock in the sanctity of our bodies and our names and identities that we would auction them off? Are we so attached to a status symbol that we would go to our grave clutching that which apparently best identified who we were and what we were about?

As it turns out, who you are is either up for sale or sold already. In our world today, everything and everyone, tragically, has a price.

Let's look now at the underlying dimension that drives so many of our purchases: namely, the belief that in buying things we establish our identity and thus find meaning. Money has become a determiner of personhood. Who one is, their worth and value and contribution to society and history, is measured solely by what they have. Regardless of whether it was earned in virtuous or in dehumanizing ways, money has a way of making us believe that with it and its influence, we are as fully human as we can be. In fact, we seem to suppose as a culture that if someone has enough money, there is barely a need to ask any questions at all. Money is the answer to everything, isn't it?

When money and the status it affords is a goal in itself, we can be assured that we have bought into a lie, an illusion. If money is the goal of life, then its fierce grip holds us captive to an identity so tied to consumption that we barely have room to breathe or space to think of ourselves outside of those terms.

If we are consumers first, then we have forgotten that, as humans, we are made in God's gift-giving image.

Consumers First

Recently my oldest daughter, Semeia, had a minor surgery. My wife and I managed to awake, predawn, to take our daughter to the hospital, where she would undergo three hours of complicated dental reconstruction. When we arrived at the hospital we were barely cognizant. Lord only knows how we managed to drive while half asleep. But when I walked into the hospital waiting room, I noticed a sign that snapped me to fully awake attention.

The sign read, "Notice to Consumers: Medical Doctors Are Licensed and Regulated by the Medical Board of California."

Did you catch it? If you didn't, read it once more. Did you notice the language used? My daughter, in this instance, was going to spend three hours under the knife in a reputable hospital not as a patient but, according to this sign, as a "consumer." What has a society come to when people have moved from being patients in need of medical care to consumers in need of medical goods? My daughter, barely old enough to

62

speak a full sentence, had already been interpreted as and assigned the title "consumer." This has taken place without any refusal on behalf of people who were once called patients, because in all honesty, most of us have calmly allowed ourselves to be described as consumers without fear, fight, or frustration. *Consumer* describes not merely our habits but what we have become.

The term *consumer* has become an identity marker that is socially acceptable for all people, from youngest to oldest. Taken further, who we actually are, as understood by our consumerist society, is manifestly related to what we buy, own, or invest in. Thus our search for love and meaning and true self-knowledge is rarely thought of as a journey that can take place outside of the marketplace. Taken to the extreme, consumers have traded love for pleasure, meaning for money, self-knowledge for self-gratification, and a life of contribution for a life of consumption. A society built on consumption is a society where people define themselves by what they devour.

From Substance to Symbol

What is the "American Dream"? We've all heard of it. James Truslow Adams once defined it as "life should be better and richer and fuller for everyone, with opportunity for each according to his ability or achievement."[7] Today, this has morphed into a culture of entitlement. Everyone should be able to own a home and a car (or two or three), and have all of the comforts "necessary" to be happy and whole.

The American Dream, in the minds of consumers, is thought of as a right, not a privilege. Why? Because consumption is what defines us and shapes our search for meaning. We have the right to be "happy." To be a consumer is to have a desire for self-expression and self-preservation that is formed by the status of what we have and own—to the degree that if we lose our stuff, our job, or our social status, our sense of self and security begins to wobble like a drunken person standing on one leg. Therefore, we try to collect and amass as much as we can to guarantee ourselves a secure place among others.

Just think about how you feel when you have money burning a hole in your pocket and the item that you have wanted for so long is now going to be yours. What meaning does it give you? Is it a mere addition to your closet or home, or does this purchase add value to you as a person? The image of Gollum from the Lord of the Rings series comes to mind, as he clasps his hands tightly around the ring of power, repeating the eerie phrase, "My precious."

Consumers have moved from purchasing items to meet a practical need to securing a symbolic status that guarantees associations they hold dear. Consumers are trained to think of themselves as unique individuals who think for themselves, who can buy whatever they want, and who make their own way in the world to the degree that "anything that would violate our right to think for ourselves, judge for ourselves, make our own decisions, live our lives as we see fit, is not only morally wrong, it is sacrilegious."[8]

Yet the incredible irony is that we buy things not as an attempt to be secure in ourselves as rugged individualists but to be part of elite communities who share the same taste, style, and symbolic appeal. These communities can be made up of wealthy yuppies wearing Polo shirts and cardigans, or countercultural hipsters who buy everything secondhand, calling it "vintage." The quality, uniqueness, and cost of what you own works like a VIP pass in a consumer-driven world, providing an entrance into social spaces that we would identify as the "in" crowd.

I noticed this in a silly personal instance. My wife, who normally carries a standard but attractive everyday brand-name purse, was given, as a gift by a family member, a high-end Coach purse. This purse, made of incredibly fine leather and studded silver, must have cost hundreds of dollars. Taken aback by such an elaborate gift, my wife was initially a little nervous parading around with her high-end handbag. Eventually, though, she succumbed to the purse's appeal and made it her primary tote for daily adventures. Immediately she noticed how bits of conversation changed with friends. Women who owned similar purses sparked up lively conversation with my wife, feeling that they must share a similar outlook and station in life because they were adorned with similar hand-bags. Requests to go shopping increased in frequency. When she was in the mall or some retail store, she was approached by saleswomen who likely assumed she had money to spare based on the purse she was carrying. Unfortunately for them, they didn't know she was wedded to a lowly pastor trying to make ends meet in the Real OC.

Regardless of the reality of her economic life, what she owned was a silent statement of who she was, what circles she ran in, and what her bank statement must look like. Own-ing a Coach purse, in this instance, was not interpreted as a statement of my wife's individual taste and style but of her social status and corporate identity. She was seen as a high-end consumer, and thus part of that rare and special crowd who is known by the limit on their credit card rather than, in the words of Martin Luther King Jr., "the content of their character."

The Mysterious Middle Class

The middle class has enough money to participate in the trendy and stylish symbols of our time, but they do so at a cost not known to the superrich. They stretch their lives to break-ing points in order to play the part. The American middle class has become known around the world for its growing consumption and its decadent lifestyles, holding the world record for having the largest homes, most appliances, and most cars per household. In 2005, the average new home had a square footage of 2,434 square feet.[9] Most suburban homes built in the 1970s have an average square footage of 1,600 square feet. It is rational to conclude that these new, huge suburban homes will be bought and inhabited by members of the professional middle class. What drives this?

Could it merely be the "symbolic" power of money?

Too many of us have become a "slave to the lender" so we can experience what is projected as the good life of independence and freedom that encompasses the American Dream. Notice the incredible irony at work here. The more we "own," the more entrenched in debt we become, and all to keep the façade of a dream that for many today has become a living nightmare. Instead of being buried in Ferraris, we are buried in debt—just to keep up the act that we are of worth because we have stuff of worth. Entrenched in a world that defines who you are by what you have, many fail to experience the true freedom that comes through a deep reliance on others and ultimately on God. Those of us who are caught up in this greedy and shallow world need to hear the words of Jesus and his call to faithful dependence.

> Therefore do not be anxious, saying, "What shall we eat?" or "What shall we drink?" or "What shall we wear?" For the Gentiles seek after all these things, and your heavenly Father knows that you need them all. But seek first the kingdom of God and his righteousness, and all these things will be added to you.[10]

Jesus uses the language of anxiety in this passage to describe the status of the human heart prior to trusting fully in God's provision. Money always tops the list of causes of anxiety. Americans numbering in the millions today are being sedated with antianxiety medications. Bestselling books promise tools to manage anxiety and offer a path to peace. But these books and medications simply treat the symptoms, not the cause.

Anxiety arises in every human heart (even my own) when what we love is at risk. What shirts we should wear, how much we should weigh, or what new car we should buy are not trivial questions for most of us. Rather they fill us with anxiety. We fear the implications of making a wrong decision. Who will we offend if we do? What groups will not accept us?

Philosopher Alain de Botton, in his book *Status Anxiety*, unwraps some interesting phenomena among the super-successful. Every adult life, he says, is defined by two great love stories. The first is our quest for sexual love, which is well-known, well-charted, and certainly exploited in our culture. The second is the human quest for lo.ve from the world, and according to de Botton, that's a more secret and shameful yearning. What other people think of us, and whether we can be judged as a success or a failure in the eyes of the world, are widespread anxieties that generally go unacknowledged and unexamined. de Botton goes so far as to say the primary reason we do the jobs we do is not merely for sustenance and provision, but more for the status that a certain income gives us.

> I think there's a high degree to which status plays a role in our motivations, in our everyday working lives. A lot of what makes low-paid work difficult isn't just the low pay; it's the lack of dignity, the lack of respect that often accompanies low-paid work. Just as what makes a lot of highly paid work nice isn't just the high pay; it's also the amount of respect and dignity that tends to accompany the accumulation of wealth.[11]

Anxiety occurs when your life is formed by a desire to impress, turn on, or win over someone or some group, yet you often come up short. It is the anxiety that comes when you have to reinvent yourself to be noticed and loved. The enormous pressure to "make something of yourself" causes millions of us to approach life as nervous and as unsure as a mouse thrown into a python's cage. That nervousness is what de Botton calls status anxiety. He goes on to say, "The thing about the modern world is that it's a world that almost defines itself by the idea that status is not something that you should inherit, either high status or low status, but rather something that each new generation should create."[12]

In other words, the peace that comes with your identity firmly gripped in grace is either too good to be true or a lie altogether.

This practice of self-creation actually hurts self-understanding. Instead of asking who we really are, we instead ask how we should appear. Appearance is grounded in perception. We fear we will not appear as together or smart or good-looking in the perception of others, so we pretend to know more than we do and continually shop for just the right clothes that will enhance our best features and hide our worst flaws. How exhausting!

This is why the gospel grabs my heart to this day. Your life is not something you have to create so others will love and welcome you. Rather, your unique life is something that God has created and is inherent. Our self will only be whole when we release our pursuit of appearance and instead surrender our self to God's care.

"Thingification"

Maybe, while driving one day, you've seen a bumper sticker that reads, "The best things in life aren't things."[13] This is a cute slogan, but how many of us believe it? How many of us believe that we can discover who we are and our purpose in life apart from the things that we own or pursue?

Our society's elevation of things has resulted in the objectification of humans. Just think about how you think of the opposite sex. Isn't it hard to understand someone as a whole person nowadays? We tend to break people down into "things," bits and pieces of which we like and enjoy, while other parts we could do without.

There are internet sites where you can "create your dream girl or guy" by adjusting the features of some virtual model to your liking. If you desire a sharper jawline, adjust the image. If you want your girl to have a bigger bust and smaller waist, well, all you have to do is scroll here and adjust there, and instantaneously you have the girl of your dreams. No wonder our relationships are so fragmented!

This outlook on attractiveness would not be as frightening if it was just some eccentric practice done in the world of cyberspace. The sad fact, though, is that it isn't. Virtual reality has merely become an expression of reality itself. A society that turns everyone into a "thing" creates consumers that, like visual cannibals, view others by their valuable parts while discarding the rest. When this takes place, we can be assured that our lives have become trivialized. They have ceased to be lives that holistically represent the image of our Creator. We can sell our foreheads and souls and baby names, because in the end these are merely things for sale.

Scripture never speaks of human beings as objects. Scripture speaks of humans as beings of incredible, innate worth. Human life ought to be marked by and belong to no one else but God. This is why the apostle Paul reminds us, "Do you not know that your bodies are temples of the Holy Spirit, who is in you, whom you have received from God? You are not your own; you were bought at a price. Therefore honor God with your bodies."[14]

What God buys through Jesus's sacrifice is the gift he first gave us when he made us in his image, before we tarnished that gift by sin, and the comfort that comes with knowing we are God's poetry. What God buys for us is the freedom to be his creation once again. We do not belong to ourselves, because we do not have the power in ourselves to fulfill the most pressing longings of our souls. Our desires to be loved and to belong, to be an individual as well as part of a community, to create and explore, are all beautiful reflections of what it means to belong to God. When God liberates us with the precious blood of his Son, he frees us from the exhausting rat race of being someone we are not. He frees us to be his and his alone, and by doing so makes us an adopted son or daughter rather than a thing up for sale.

Dietrich Bonhoeffer sums this up nicely when he writes:

> The real man is at liberty to be his Creator's creature. To be conformed with the incarnate is to have the right to be the man one really is. Now there is no more pretence, no more hypocrisy

or self-violence, no more compulsion to be something other, better and more ideal that what one is. God loves the real man.[15]

God loves the real man, woman, and child as he created them, and when you believe this and live your life by it, you will be free from being a *thing*, and all that goes along with a life of consumption. What you own or consume is purposed to give you the ability to add your divine spark to the wildfire of God's work in the world. To settle for a cheap association with the money you make or don't make or the things you have or don't have is to toss the pearl of great price and hold on to a grain of dirt.

Questions for Reflection

The Scriptures say that the "love of money is a root of all kinds of evil."[16] Why do you think money can lead to so much harm?

Does money play more of a practical or symbolic role in your life? For instance, do you identify yourself as a person in relationship to what you have?

Have you ever felt the effects of status anxiety? What compels us to care so much about the opinions of others in terms of what we make or have?

Is there a limit to what you would do for money, or does everything and everyone really have a price?

4

Google Stole My Brain

There was a time when maps did not exist, and in those times traveling was done intuitively. Landmarks were memorized, rivers and trees became symbols that separated safe roads from dangerous ones. Traveling far in a world without maps was risky, and done with a certain amount of blind faith and courage, but ultimately done out of necessity. Yet with the birth of maps humans took hold of their natural environment and gradually fractured it into a thousand provinces, shires, countries, states, highways, and byways.

Mapmaking has changed throughout history. The earliest maps charted the heavens as a way of understanding the world below. Religion had a huge impact on mapmaking. Jerusalem in the Middle Ages, for instance, was noted to be the center of the world, the home of God. Later, maps changed according to rulers and empires. Wars literally redrew the boundaries and required new maps for new territories.

Seeing the world in terms of countries and states with borders has become so intuitive that we have forgotten these markers are not a part of the actual, natural landscape. Maps evolve as humans shape history.

Through our maps, we willingly become a part of their boundaries. If our home is included, we feel pride, perhaps familiarity, but always a sense that *this is ours*. If it is not, we accept our roles as outsiders, though we may be of the same mind and culture. In this way, maps can be dangerous and powerful tools.[1]

Like all tools, maps have the potential to be used for good or ill. One thing is for certain, maps have changed the ways humans think about their world and will no doubt continue to shape and reshape how we see the landscapes of our lives as maps are redrawn and re-formed. Are maps something that shape our minds and lives so deeply that, though we have created them, they actually have created us? One wonders.

Clocks, like maps, have also become an indispensable human invention. Before clocks, time was marked by the sun and moon alone. Sundials were used to determine the time of day based on the height of the sun and its corresponding brightness. The minute hand, essential to early mechanical clocks, was not conceived until 1577. Jost Burgi devised the minute hand as part of a clock made for Tycho Brahe, an astronomer who needed an accurate measurement of time for his investigation of the stars. It was not uncommon for homes in the sixteenth century to be equipped only with sundials to tell the time.

The minute clock made time more precise and soon began changing significant dynamics of human behavior. To precisely measure time means to measure all of life with more detail. This is not in itself a bad thing; we can merely make the observation that with the birth of the minute hand and progress in the art of timekeeping, human life was reorganized and changed by yet another one of its inventions. And in our day and age, thinking in terms of minutes has become antiquated. We can measure seconds and milliseconds, reducing time to mind-numbing specificity. World records are defended or broken in seconds or tenths of seconds. This ability to measure time so precisely has moved us from being keepers of time to now, in some ways, being kept by time.

So, what do maps and clocks have to do with our true selves? What do these two common technologies have to teach us about living a life based on trivial pursuits? More than you might think. New technologies that become commonplace actually shape our brains, rewiring our understanding of reality. As newer technologies become increasingly intuitive to our everyday lives, could we, over time, lose our essential self, our soul, and our ability to think, reason, and engage the world with wonder? Think about your own life for a moment. Have you grown impatient when it comes to learning about and processing the complexities of life? Or have you grown tired of the long-winded options that compete for our intellectual devotion? We will fail to achieve all we have the potential to achieve if our intellectual capacities continue to be weakened by mental outsourcing.

Could Google be stealing our brains?

Neuroscientists and scholars who have devoted their own minds and time to understand the brain have discovered some fascinating characteristics. Among the most peculiar features of the brain is what scholars call neuroplasticity.[2] What this means is that the brain is not static. It does not just grow and develop for a time and then stop. The brain is always absorbing new information, and this information changes the actual physical structure of the brain. New pathways are carved as new information is inputted. Habits shape the brain's structure. This is why driving down a familiar road or doing your morning routine takes little brain energy, if any, because what has become routine has been engraved in your brain.

With the invention of maps and clocks, our brains were gradually rewired. The gray mush that is a mystery to all of us is not as far from play dough as we might imagine. We are able to shape our brains in unique ways that create habits, hang-ups, addictions, or perfections of skills that were not innate at birth. Another way of thinking about this is that our brains become formed by what we experience, believe, and do.

With every scientific discovery there comes a business opportunity. This is certainly true with the discovery of neuroplasticity. The website www.lumosity.com is the first of its kind. Boasting a growing twenty-five-million-member community, Lumosity.com is a website built upon recent studies in neuroscience. According to the website,

> Lumo Labs has used this cutting-edge science to create a set of web-based software tools that empower people to exercise their brains and achieve their maximum performance. The assessments, games, and training courses on the Lumosity website are based on real science and are presented in an appealing, engaging form that makes it fun to exercise the brain.[3]

What the site essentially offers is "cognitive exercise." They claim "cognitive exercise is like physical exercise: anyone can benefit, regardless of age, gender, profession, or educational background."[4] The site promises that "drawing on the newest developments in neuroscience, Lumosity.com offers brain-training exercises that work. Regardless of your age, Lumosity can make you smarter and more mentally fit."[5]

Those in the scientific community, along with the millions of members of Lumosity.com, have discovered something that we all in some ways know to be true. We have adaptable brains. Ways of thinking get strengthened or weakened by our habits. Changes in technology have the suspicious ability to rewire our brains. Maps, clocks, and now iPads, cell phones, e-tablets, and daily new additions to the technological landscape, many fueled by the all-powerful internet, share one thing in common: they all wield influential, shaping power over the human brain. Like Frankenstein's monster, the creation has now become more powerful than the creator, and the implications for the human brain are immeasurable.

The "Googlization" of our society, the overdependence on and saturation of the internet, is altering the human brain. The long-term effects of this are stark and potentially detrimental to the very uniqueness that makes us human and divine image bearers. Not all of the effects are bad, but certainly they are not all benign. Some carry malignancies that can decay the human imagination and trivialize the human spirit. This may not alarm people who believe progress always carries with it its victims, but it should alarm those who claim the name of Jesus. Christians are called to love God with all of our minds. What we set our minds to is an act of worship. The apostle Paul understands, in part, worship of God as the "renewal of our minds."[6] Therefore our brains matter to God.

Short Circuit

As a child of the '80s I was raised on a steady diet of comedic science fiction films that satirized the unexpected effects of new technologies. *Short Circuit*, a 1986 film about a military robot with heart and soul, is one of my favorites. "Johnny 5," the name assigned it by the military, comes to life through a freak incident—alive in mind and heart, alive in emotion, and desiring to become more human with each passing day. Johnny 5 craves information. He would read through encyclopedic volumes in a matter of seconds. One of the funniest scenes in the film is when the robot tears apart a home to find "more input." Addicted to acquiring new bits of information, Johnny 5 slowly becomes more humanized via his newly formed understanding of the world. His characteristic catchphrase "more input" is part of his process of becoming more than a machine.

Humans are a bit like Johnny 5 in this way. We search, Google, download, buy, and store away as much input as our minds and hard drives can store. We are forever on the hunt for the newest widget or app or tidbit of knowledge. We are hunters of technologies and gatherers of information. The only problem is, unlike Johnny 5, we are not robots when it comes to gathering information. Our minds, as neuroplasticity shows, are ever adapting to the information we're storing and processing. Our brains have to choose what is important or trivial. It does this through mechanisms we are not cognitively aware of. Your brain goes about filing away or discarding old information so that new bits of information can be stored. It is a matter of research as to whether we actually do lose this "old" information. Our brains are being shaped by new technologies that are creating new ways of storing information, and it is the type of information we store and how we store it that, in many ways, makes us distinctly human.

None of us would be the same without our special set of memories that provide the narrative arc for our lives. Our memories make us, shape us, and create us into the people we are today. The ability to patiently and meticulously sort through experiences is part of the joy and sorrow that make human life unique and worth living. Yet our brains are being reshaped in such ways that some of the most prized abilities that have propelled us to our greatest discoveries are being outsourced. For instance, we don't have to remember anything anymore.

As a child, I remember the joy of learning my home phone number. I forget how old I was exactly, but I remember experiencing a sense of pride, of feeling "older" because I could recite my phone number. New technologies have replaced my need to remember my phone number and the phone numbers of others. I still remember a time when I knew all the important numbers of friends and family by heart. Now I am dependent on my cell phone. And maybe it is a wonderful thing that we have outsourced our memory, seeing as we can now make room for more significant information. Yet is this happening? Are new technologies making us smarter and more sophisticated in our "knowing," or are they making it easier for our minds to know less and therefore become dull?

In his book *The Shallows: What the Internet Is Doing to Our Brains*, Pulitzer Prize nominee Nicholas Carr offers a profound rendering of what is happening to the human brain in our internet-dependent society. One of his primary concerns is the long-term effects on humans if the trend of digital outsourcing continues. He writes,

> We don't constrain our mental powers when we store new long-term memories. We strengthen them. With each expansion of our memory comes an enlargement of our intelligence. The Web provides a convenient and compelling supplement to personal memory—but when we start using the Web as a substitute for personal memory, by bypassing the inner processes of consolidation, we risk emptying our minds of their riches.[7]

One of the ways people historically have sharpened and perfected their memory and brainpower is through reading. Reading, the uninterrupted attention to simple words on paper, shapes the mind and memory to be diligent, patient, sharp, and focused. Compare this to browsing on the internet where distraction is part of the learning game. Instead of sitting without distraction, the internet is built for distraction. It is designed as a flashing advertisement billboard that gets you to "browse" here, "click" there, and "surf" everywhere. In his *Atlantic* article provocatively titled "Is Google Making Us Stupid?" Carr cites a study on how people used the internet for research and study:

> They found that people using the sites exhibited "a form of skimming activity," hopping from one source to another and rarely returning to any source they'd already visited. They typically read no more than one or two pages of an article or book before they would "bounce" out to another site. Sometimes they'd save a long article, but there's no evidence that they ever went back and actually read it. The authors of the study report: It is clear that users are not reading online in the traditional sense; indeed there are signs that new forms of "reading" are emerging as users "power browse" horizontally through titles, contents pages and abstracts going for quick wins. It almost seems that they go online to avoid reading in the traditional sense.[8]

"Reading in the traditional sense." It is hard to even know what that means anymore. One can hardly imagine a generation raised on multiple media devices, twitter alerts and updates, and a constant onslaught of texts and social media assaults being able to sit down with Fyodor Dostoevsky's *The Brothers Karamazov* or Saint Augustine's *Confessions*—not to mention the Bible that billions refer to as holy. In a world of immediate intellectual satisfaction, the result is intellectual stupefaction. Carr, a brilliant thinker in his own right, offers a personal account of his own mental metamorphosis. His words mirror my own experience, and the experience of many people I know:

> Over the last few years I've had an uncomfortable sense that someone, or something, has been tinkering with my brain, remapping the neural circuitry, reprogramming the memory. My mind isn't going—so far as I can tell—but it's changing. I'm not thinking the way I used to think. I feel it most strongly when I'm reading. I used to find it easy to immerse myself in a book or lengthy article. . . . Now my concentration starts to drift after a page or two. I get fidgety, lose the thread, and begin looking for something else to do. I feel like I'm always dragging my wayward brain back to the text. The deep reading that used to come naturally has become a struggle.[9]

Could it be that our world is shaping us all with attention deficit disorder? We have given over parts of our brains to smart machines, and the result of this outsourcing could be that we are making ourselves dumber.

Data Smog

Journalist David Shenk invented the term "data smog" to refer to the overwhelming amount of information at our fingertips. "Let us call this unexpected, unwelcome part of our atmosphere 'data smog' as an expression for the noxious muck and druck of the information age. Data smog gets in the way; it crowds out quiet moments, and obstructs much-needed contemplation. It spoils conversation, literature, and even entertainment."[10] The benefit of the internet is that information that once was only accessible to a select class of people is now made available to the masses. I too believe this has brought much benefit.

My concern is for those of us in oversaturated societies such as America where the vast amount of information we are exposed to in a day will create apathy among us in the quest for truth. We slowly give more and more parts of our brain over to machines because of their accessibility and in doing so become something different, something potentially less human. Unable to discern truth from fiction, substance from symbol, or poetry from propaganda, our minds that should be searching for what matters most instead are prone to seek that which comes easiest or with the best marketing pitch. In fact, according to statistics provided by Shenk, "In 1971 the average American was targeted by at least 560 daily advertisement messages. Twenty years later, that number has risen sixfold, to 3,000 messages per day."[11] We have become used to communicating information in quips and tweets.

According to research done at the University of California at San Diego, the average person during a normal day views 34 gigabytes of data and 100,500 words. The study also showed that we are now exposed to 11.8 hours of information each day, calculated by the amount of information flowing into American households.[12]

Data smog indeed!

Why does this matter, practically speaking?

I approach this not as a disinterested academic who lives high above the real world in an ivory tower but as a pastor. And I'm a pastor who has lived most of my adult life among thousands of people searching for meaning and rarely finding it. I see, daily, the lives and minds of young people of all types who find it difficult, if not impossible, to land with confidence on what they believe and why. Not only that, I am a father. My children will be raised in a world that will have an even greater dependence on technologies to "think for them." Automating and outsourcing our minds will only increase, and the results for the church and the message of Jesus is alarming.

One of the results of a world with greater data smog complexity is what I call "decide-aphobia," the fear of making decisions, or more particularly the wrong decision. Faced with millions upon millions of options, many of us have "analysis paralysis" when it comes to making decisions. Some of these decisions are trivial, such as what to wear and where to eat. Others are more important, such as where to go to college or what to do for a career. Some of these questions are of utmost—dare I say eternal—importance. Is there a God? Which is the right God? There are so many religions, which one is right? It is not surprising that the generation with more options than ever is also the one that is the most relativistic in their thinking. Complexity leads to relativism. There's even a word for this—*complexification*.

The fastest growing religious group in America are the "nones," the nonreligious. These, as we have noted earlier, are people who are indifferent to all religions or identify as "spiritual but not religious." Could their indifference be driven by the staggering complexity of the world as it exists today? Maybe the search for truth seems exhausting, and it is just easier to make no decision than to make an informed decision. In a world of fast-paced images, Google searches, and short tweets, there is an intolerance for deep introspection and investigating, which ensures that the quickest and most easily understood image or slogan wins the minds and hearts of people. Because of the fast pace of our viral world, people are less interested in introspection of any sort, preferring to give their lives to whatever product or party can be packaged with media savvy.

Outsourcing introspection like this will lead to debilitating consequences. When truth is replaced with convenience, current cultural icons hold more power to transform the human spirit than time-tested sources of beautiful truths such as those found in Christianity. When Lady Gaga is more quotable than Jesus, culture has reached a spiritual and moral crisis that is potentially catastrophic for the world and the church. When laziness, the impulse to know without knowing, overwhelms the great human quest of understanding, cheap slogans and propaganda will seem more palatable and real simply because they are more easily digestible. Knowledge may be disregarded for exhibition, resulting in a society where packaging and advertising win out over substance and truth. Surely this process of having our brains stolen won't take place overnight, but if we don't prioritize and value a desire for truth, it is only a matter of time until our minds are hijacked and reshaped by machines that do the thinking for us.

Now What?

So what am I saying, really? That we should throw away our computers and smartphones and return to excavating dusty card catalogs and microfiche archives? No, not in the least. I am not so naïve as to think that we are able to or should simply move back in time to some utopian universe of yesteryear. Such a utopia has never existed, and as concerned as I am about some of the effects of our connected world, nostalgia is not an attribute I'm prone to dabble in. But we would be more than naïve to not understand the unique and staggering changes peculiar to our generation. So, then, what should be our approach to loving God with our minds in the world we live in?

Seeking truth must be a Christian endeavor. We mustn't be so stunned by or caught up in "data fog" that we fail to make our way through the tough terrain that leads from disarray to discovering truth. In an era of information gluttony, we must show patience and temperance in our quest to know the "truth that shall set us free."[13] Impatience is a sin. Temperance is a virtue, it is the ability to measure decisions by their long-term impact. It means using restraint and carefully weighing the options before making a decision. Coming to a conclusion through temperance means you have spent time evaluating the benefits and value of the statements being made and the truths within them. Yes, it will take time to discover truth in this way, but what happens if you fail to take the time to do so? Could it be that you will joyfully live your life within the guise of a lie? Scary as it seems, this is not an uncommon thing.

Some of us are so committed to avoiding the cost of searching that we remain stuck in apathy and confusion. There is truth out there—real, beautiful, and thoughtful ways of seeing reality and even knowing God, if we dare to try. Some of us will use doubt as a mask of confidence to hide our confusion. As Dallas Willard has quipped, "For centuries now our culture has cultivated the idea that the skeptical person is always smarter than one who believes. You can almost be as stupid as a cabbage as long as you doubt."[14] In a society that cultivates doubt as a virtue, skepticism can be a cheap drink to numb the confusion of questioning the meaning of it all. We must remain sober in our search.

The church must also regain its place in the public intellectual arena. The last place our secular world would look for thought-provoking, disciplined, and focused people is the church. The church has been ridiculed and devalued as a machine that is operated by playing with people's emotions, the supposedly weaker part of our minds. Manipulation and false promises stir congregations into an unintellectual frenzy, so they say, and preachers and pastors are the medicine men who bewitch the minds of millions. Though I find this view to be largely stereotypical, I do have a bone to pick with the way the church, in large part, devalues learning.

In his famous and controversial book *The Scandal of the Evangelical Mind*, historian Mark Noll writes,

> The scandal of the evangelical mind is that there is not much of an evangelical mind. . . . Despite dynamic success at a

popular level, modern American evangelicals have failed notably in sustaining serious intellectual life. They have nourished millions of believers in the simple verities of the gospel but have largely abandoned the universities, the arts, and other realms of "high" culture.[15]

I cannot agree with Noll more.

Birthed out of this agreement is my conviction that the church and its leadership must take advantage of the time we live in and hold on to ancient ways of gaining knowledge. We must refuse the easy decision to outsource our brain to technology. What would the world be like if it progressed along its chosen path, giving more and more of its mind away, and the only people who read large books, studied cultural artifacts of the past, and produced discoveries in the sciences were those who took the command to "love God with their mind" seriously? Maybe our influence in culture would be deeper and wider than it is today. This would require the church to highlight learning as an essential part of spirituality. We will say more about this later, but for now, let me say that the church housed knowledge for hundreds of years. This knowledge birthed the world we live in today. Could the church be the womb for a renaissance of learning in a world that is continually having its brain stolen? I think so.

To fulfill this mission, we must appoint intellectual curators among us, men and women who will dedicate themselves to study in an accountable way so they can serve as reliable resources and models of Christian learning for the congregation. I believe every church should have a full-time theologian on staff whose only job is to study, teach, publish, and serve as an intellectual resource and model for learning. Imagine if the four hundred thousand churches in America made supplying the public with Christian intellectuals part of their programs?

We need to actively combat our tendency toward letting the internet "know" for us. We need to be willing to do the hard work of memorization, diligent study, and patient and temperate investigation. If we do, we may stop Google from stealing our brains.

Questions for Reflection

Have you noticed the effects of outsourcing your brain? Has dependence on the internet affected the way you think or the rate at which you learn?

How has the internet benefitted or hindered the search for human meaning?

Do you find that you and others are more sure about what is true, good, and beautiful in the world in light of the "Googlization" of our world, or are you less sure about such things?

Do you consider Christianity a religion primarily of the heart or of the mind?

What could Christians do to cultivate the life of the mind in their churches?

5

What's Your Status?

The earth has a remarkable history. Learning about the migration of the continents was especially interesting to me as a child. I still remember seeing the illustrated map of Pangaea, the one massive continent that seemingly held together the earth's landmasses. Surrounded by water alone, Pangaea was a unified raft where the continents clasped one another's hands to assemble one landmass where life could flourish. Yet all good things must come to an end, and so was the case with Pangaea. As our current maps show, the continents fissured and like floating puzzle pieces moved far from their original connectedness.

Pangaea means "entire earth," a word that speaks of unity rather than separation. What has become of Pangaea symbolizes for me a troublesome feeling that we have lost something we can no longer recover. We long for togetherness, but when we look at the map of our lives, the continents have shifted. Far distant lands across expansive oceans are our reality. Yet the longing for our own "Pangaea" is still there, and its yearning pokes its head up every so often, especially in our innate human desire for connection.

From birth, every child longs to remain connected with his or her mother or caregiver. Babies crave nurture, and even before they can fully see in color, and far before they can utter even the simplest thought aloud, there is an urgent and undeniable longing to be with another. The distance created by normal and routine times of separation is painful. This pain is present and evident in the raw emotion expressed in a child's cry in the absence of his or her mother. There in the cry is a longing for Pangaea. Yet the child is reared to be increasingly separate from the mother as days and weeks go by. This acceptance of separation does not come easily or immediately.

Jacques Lacan, a famous thinker in the field of psycho-analysis, believed in the "mirror stage" of childhood development. Lacan's mirror stage is based on the belief that when infants first see themselves in a mirror, they have no real sense of being a separate person from another until, at the earliest, six months of age. Their reflection in the mirror fascinates them, but there is no sign that this fascination means they sense they are a unique being apart from the connection they have to their caregivers.

Lacan's research also showed that, although children are fascinated with images of themselves and others in mirrors from about six months of age, they do not begin to recognize that the images in the mirror are reflections of their own bodies until the age of about fifteen to eighteen months. Pause and think about this for a moment. We are created in the body of another, brought to full form in the womb of another, and yet delivered into this world as a separate person, complete with a name, birth certificate, and Social Security number. We are a separate person thrown into an alien world.

To be a person is to begin by being intimately connected to another for our care and provision. Unable to even recognize ourselves as "ourselves" in the mirror for over a year, our sense of independence grows gradually as time moves on. We must learn to experience the slow and gradual continental drift of life as we progress in days and wisdom. We must become independent, self-reliant, our own man or woman taking hold of our life in the world.

Especially for those raised in America, independence is the single virtue that liberates us from the naïve and child-like longings for Pangaea. As time goes on for children, they learn to become more independent, more fully "themselves."

I remember the first time I got a taste of independence. I must have been nine or ten years old when I was invited by a friend a few years older than me to ride our bikes two miles away to get some candy. When I asked my mother, I braced myself for a thunderous no, but to my shock she said yes. Her permission terrified me. Given some precautionary words of wisdom from my mother, my string of safety and dependence began to tear. One bike ride eventually turned into a driver's license, which morphed into me living on my own. My journey of independence, of self-discovery, of being an individual making his way into the world had begun.

One of the earliest ways we inaugurate independence is through the discovery of likes and dislikes, personal gifts and weaknesses, and overall temperament. Having three children under the age of four, my daily life is an exploration into the unique likes and dislikes of growing children. The individual fingerprint is obvious from an early age. There comes a time, though, where what is intuitive naturally transforms into a journey to "know thyself." The question of ourselves is one of the oldest quests of the human spirit.

"To thine own self be true" is a slogan that rings of liberty and freedom from the shackles of others' opinions and ways of life. Over time we become so detached from others in the discovery of our self that emotional and mental health are expressed in independence. This freedom, we are told, is life. It is this liberation from others that is the highest good. Isn't it? Or are there signs that the continents have shifted—but in their wake have left a deep and pervading sense of separation that, at times, disrupts our self-reliant stride? Has our ride of independence taken us off route? Are we less independent than we imagine?

Maybe it is when we take a stroll through family photo albums and view smiles we did not know our faces were capable of making as we sit in our mother's arms. Or it could be when we drive by our old schoolyard and envision the endless hours spent playing on swing sets, or hide and seek with friends of days past. We feel a phantom overtake us, a memory, a subtle reminder of a world that was and is no longer. Rarely were the good old days spent alone. Most of the greatest memories we have are ones of shared memories and experiences. Yet again and again we are told to be ourselves, to take our own path and, like Sinatra, "do it my way." Yet self-discovery does not lead to ultimate satisfaction.

Every person experiences a longing for Pangaea, especially in the face of loss. When death's grip clutches the life of someone we love, the fissure between unity and division deepens. Pangaea is longed for. Hoped for. Mourned over. Death reminds us that the independence many of us are raised to praise as the highest good is a carefully crafted cover-up of the truth that we are attached to others in ways that are beautifully unspeakable. When we lose someone we love, all of the slogans and propaganda of independence dissolve into moans. We are stretched by our longing for Pangaea once again and reminded of how far away from it we are.

I suspect that the slogans and attempts to live in complete independence from others is a bandage to cover a deep yet concealed wound. A longing for Pangaea, if you will.

With every new generation, there are unique insights into who we are as people. The rise of social media, Facebook in particular, is a cultural event of such significance that its total impact is hard to measure. With over one billion of the earth's inhabitants active on Facebook, its universal appeal and influence is undoubtedly second to none. It has become the epicenter for communication among younger generations and will no doubt continue to evolve and splinter into new uses with new audiences growing daily.

Why has social media like Facebook become so immensely popular? What are the forces that brought social media to the marketplace, and why has social media struck such a nerve with so many people? Facebook may trivialize our lives more than we suppose, but it only does so because one of our fundamental desires—connection and unity with others—has been repurposed by our virally connected world.

My Status Is Lonely

If the world is increasingly more connected, the result should be that humans are having their innate desire for intimacy with others met in a greater way. But in fact, many argue, the opposite is occurring.

Stephen Marche sent a shudder down the social media spine in his 2012 *Atlantic* article when he asked the question "Is Facebook Making Us Lonely?"

The question is filled with irony, as the slogan of Facebook is "A place for friends." When has anyone with hundreds or (this is my moment of personal confession) thousands of friends become lonely? Loneliness is reserved for those who are withdrawn, "low in the face, slow in the race" type losers who find it difficult to make friends. Right? Surely someone who can access a website well-crafted by their own egotism, filled with hundreds of friends, small novels of their own likes and dislikes, fan pages, and pics of weekend ragers, should have their fundamental longing for connection met. Shouldn't they? Though we are more connected, more globalized, more plugged in, and more logged on in every sphere of our existence than ever before, our basic longing for unity and connection is somehow being left unquenched.

Our forebearers would find our current way of life unfathomable. Imagine a family living in the mountains of Montana or the deserts of Arizona one hundred years ago. Our world is so different and distinct from one century ago that it would not be hyperbole to declare that we indeed live in a new world. Take the telephone, for instance. Telephone usage was limited to a very few people, and only those who had the wealth could own a phone and operate it as part of their normal routine. The very thought of international communication, video communication, the internet, Skype, Facetime, and the plethora of other communication means and devices we have at our disposal would be science fiction to those living in the early twentieth century. Their ability to connect was limited, but were their relationships? As Marche illustrates with brilliance,

> We are living in an isolation that would have been unimaginable to our ancestors, and yet we have never been more accessible. Over the past three decades, technology has delivered to us a world in which we need not be out of contact for a fraction of a moment. In 2010, at a cost of $300 million, 800 miles of fiber-optic cable was laid between the Chicago Mercantile Exchange and the New York Stock Exchange to shave three milliseconds off trading times. Yet within this world of instant and absolute communication, unbounded by limits of time or space, we suffer from unprecedented alienation. We have never been more detached from one another, or lonelier. In a world consumed by ever more novel modes of socializing, we have less and less actual society. We live in an accelerating contradiction: the more connected we become, the lonelier we are. We were promised a global village; instead we inhabit the drab cul-de-sacs and endless freeways of a vast suburb of information.[1]

The main culprit is social media, and as the title of his article suggests, more specifically Facebook. Before unpacking the strength of Marche's argument, we must be clear on what he is not saying: he is not saying that Facebook is somehow responsible for the loneliness in our lives. He is not saying that with the advent of social media humans have become slaves to loneliness, oppressed by the meticulous and cunning marketing techniques of Mark Zuckerberg and his army of totalitarian trailblazers. "Casting technology as some vague, impersonal spirit of history forcing our actions is a weak excuse. We make decisions about how we use our machines, not the other way around."[2] Facebook is merely "at the forefront of all this unexpectedly lonely interactivity."[3]

According to Marche and many others, the signs of our loneliness are everywhere. "In 1950, less than 10 percent of American households contained only one person. By 2010, nearly 27 percent of households had just one person."[4]

One of the determining factors of loneliness is the quality of our interactions rather than the amount of interactions we have. Depth, not breadth, heals the wound of loneliness. Yet social media is largely gauged as a value because it exposes you to more people than you could ever have meaningful conversations with in real life. Some people collect baseball cards, others Facebook friends and Twitter followers. The saying "he who dies with the most toys wins" has surely been challenged by "he who dies with the most friends wins," even if these "friends" are people you have never met nor care to meet.

In 2010 filmmaker Katherine Brooks solicited supporters over an online fund-raising site called Kickstarter for a proposed documentary she wished to make titled *Face 2 Face*. Katherine wanted to make a film that chronicled the relationship between loneliness and social media. "How can I have 5,000 friends on Facebook and feel alone? Are there other people in the world that feel this way? Do we spend more time with technology than we do each other? Why, when I'm out at dinner, do I see people who are face to face, but on their phones tweeting, texting, Facebooking?"[5]

Face 2 Face chronicles a three-month journey in which Katherine attempted to meet fifty of her Facebook friends whom she had met only online. These fifty people were chosen when she posted a status update on her Facebook page that asked who was willing to spend a day with her and she would come to them and film the whole process. At the end of her project, the six most profound stories of the fifty were chosen and edited into a feature-length documentary.

In an interview at the Newport Beach film festival, Katherine explored the reasons that motivated her to make the film.

> I was recovering from surgery and went into a very deep depression. I wasn't happy with my career or my personal life and I wanted a change. I had literally felt as though I had hit a brick wall and was ready to give up on life. That was when I was staring at my Facebook page in tears and looking at how many friends I had, yet I felt so alone and disconnected from the world. It was in that moment I really had an intense awakening that if I was at a point in my life where I was ready to throw in the towel, I might as well do something that scared me . . . to connect with people face to face.[6]

Can we hear the hushed echo, the quiet longing for "Pangaea" in Katherine's words? I believe so. I also believe she is not unique. Many of us are filled with the ironic sense that though we have collected friends like antiques, we fear we are unknown, unloved, lost in a sea of human traffic. Could it be possible that if we were really honest with ourselves, the next time we log on to Facebook and are asked to give a status update we could type "I am lonely"? We publicize our life to the world in order to affirm to ourselves that it might matter to someone. With every like or tag or comment, our need for connection is being met—but is it really? Could it be that though we are centralized and together on Facebook, we are altogether separate?

Altogether Separate

All of us learn to hide bits of ourselves from others. Whether to call this natural I am not sure, but it is certainly normal. This is what makes getting to know someone significant. To really feel that you have access to another person's inner world is a gift beyond measure and comes only through time and patience. Opening ourselves up to one another is terrifying. We fear rejection. We contemplate our weaknesses and what others will think when they discover we are less like Hercules and more like the Cowardly Lion. As a result, much of our time is focused on presenting a mask to others. A problem occurs, what psychologists commonly call the creation of a false self, when the mask becomes more real than the reality. When the mask, the false self, is all we know, all we show, and all we live by, what happens to the real person behind the mask?

Does social media encourage people to be themselves, their true selves, or does it encourage the creation of a false persona. Are we becoming a generation of false selves?

Dr. Jim Taylor, a renowned psychologist, has written much on the role of social media and the impact it has had on the identity of adolescents. In one of his more famous pieces he asks the question, "Is Facebook creating a false self in your children?"[7] Dr. Taylor writes and speaks frequently on the normal formation of personality. In particular he writes on the formation of the self through internal or external factors. Internal factors are the immediate social connections the child engages in, such as family, close friends, teachers, and religious leaders. These factors have been the primary influences in shaping the values and behaviors of children and youth for generations. Another way to think about internal factors is that these are the influences that the child or adolescent can engage with face-to-face. They typically live in close proximity.

External factors, on the other hand, typically take the form of media within popular culture and are considered secondary to the primary psychological forces that shape a child's identity. The ability to discern what is right from wrong or valuable or invaluable has usually been shaped by the most local and present influences in a person's life. Yet there has been a shift in our world. According to Dr. Taylor, our culture has become so enamored and influenced by "external" forces that we are shaping the psyche of our children in potentially harmful ways.

> ·The result of this externalization may be your children developing a *false self*, in which they internalize the messages of popular culture and media, such as valuing themselves based on their wealth, appearance, or popularity, and those messages become the foundation of their self-identity. . . . The false self is constructed to satisfy the needs of popular culture, in particular, to generate more profit for those companies that control popular culture. Its emphasis on those needs, for example, materialism, physical appearance, popularity, and celebrity, results in children feeling psychologically, emotionally, and socially "undernourished" because these aspects of the false self don't satisfy their most basic needs for love, security, competence, and connection. In the absence of real meaning and fulfillment in their lives, children become dependent on media to meet the immediate and superficial needs of the externally constructed false self that provides them with only the bare minimum of "nourishment" to survive.[8]

Dr. Taylor goes even further in diagnosing the emergence of this false self among adolescents, citing recent research on the influence of social media on the formation of false selves and the resulting insecurity and low self-esteem growing in those who are immersed in such practices.

> One study found that Facebook users who had low self-esteem posted more "self-promotional" materials on their pages than those with high self-esteem. Another study reported that those who were more dependent on outside influences for their self-esteem were more likely to spend more time and post more photos of themselves on Facebook.[9]

Our longing for connection and intimacy with others has been hijacked by a fascination with virtual community, and the result is more frequent instances of insecurity and low self-esteem evident in this generation. Think about it for a moment.

When you go to update your Facebook status, send a tweet, or post a picture on Instagram, what goes through your mind prior to doing so? Do you carefully screen the pictures that make you look thinner and more fashionable, and will draw more likes and comments than others? When asked, "How are you doing today?" do you answer with the same honesty and candor that you would if you were in the presence of a trusted friend? What about viewing the profiles and posts of others? Are there not heightened experiences of making comparisons, judging other's behavior, or feeling insecure about your own life? When friendship is based on our ability to personally brand ourselves in order to get the approval of others, loneliness is a natural result.

For those who spend more time in virtual community than in real flesh-and-blood relationships, the slide from truth to fiction should be a genuine concern. In real community you can't just "block" or "delete" an argument or a disagreement and be done with it. If interaction with others is in person, things are much messier than that, aren't they? In real community, narcissism does damage to relationships, whereas in the virtual world, narcissism and self-worship are simply called marketing.

Are we creating a generation of people who are learning how to brand themselves more than they are learning to find themselves? Are we trivializing real community with a virtual and viral form of superficiality that celebrates distance, fantasy, and illusion? Is our longing for unity and connection with others really being met in hours spent in front of a computer screen or scrolling on our smartphones? What is the alternative to virtual community and what will this alternative do to our sense of self and our innate longing for community? Is there a form of "life together" that enlivens rather than trivializes our search for "Pangaea"? I think there is.

The Body of Christ

We begin life in the body of another, yet there is that moment when we are told to be separate, independent, and eventually set apart from all others. Our entire life is longing to be reunited with another, and this deep longing is not a thorn in the side that God has given to us. Rather, he has given us this longing because it is an ache that leads to a better way of life.

It is not a virtual body we long for but a real one. But we are so desperate for connection that we allow our longing to satiate itself too cheaply. We want easy, immediate, uncomplicated community, and Facebook and other social media enterprises merely give us what we want. Yet this is cheap imitation and unworthy of our undivided attention. It simply doesn't measure up to what God offers us in Christ.

The church is Christ's body, literally the hands and feet and mouth and heart of Jesus, alive in the world. The gospel unabashedly proclaims that we are longing for Christ in our longing for one another. Our desire for connection, for reconnection with the body of another, is not at its core sexual but theological. We indeed are created to long for unity with another, and that other is Jesus. In Jesus's body, the church, we indeed are formed, melded, and mended into the flesh of another. We are one with Christ.

What we do with our bodies is what we do with his body, just as what a pregnant mother eats and drinks becomes part of her baby's body. As we become part of Christ, we become part of one another. The location of God's "Pangaea" is the church, where men and women of all ages, backgrounds, ethnicities, economic situations, languages, and lifestyles are brought together in the name of Christ. In belonging to Christ we belong to one another, and this unity is hard yet also rewarding, unlike the cheap and disconnected forms of community that live under the umbrella of social media.

In the church we are social because we are one, and the medium that establishes our oneness is Jesus. It is this community, this body, that has been viral and global for two thousand years. It is this community that will outlive, outlast, and out-love all other forms of community. It is this community that we are called to protect, love, serve, and proclaim.

Questions for Reflection

Has social media benefitted or hurt the depth of your relationships?

How many hours do you spend using social media a week? Does this investment of time make you feel happier as a person and closer to others?

If given the choice, would you rather have many virtual friendships or a few flesh-and-blood relationships?

Do you think social media contributes to loneliness and envy? How so? How not?

6

Holograms Don't Die

Japan is home to pop princess Hatsune Miku, a music sensation taking over the hearts and charts of both young and old in Japan. With her long indigo pigtails and her part schoolgirl, part spy style, she is an attractive and trend-setting addition to Japanese pop culture. Her voice is perfect in every way, though it sounds like it might have gone through a little—OK, a lot—of studio magic. Whatever "it" is, she's got "it" in a big way, and like many of her hot, young, and up-and-coming singer peers, Miku is profoundly fake.

Like 3-D hologram fake.[1]

Hatsune Miku was originally created as a character to sell the digital singing software created by Crypton Future Media, which customers could purchase and then program to perform any song on their computer. Crypton uses voices recorded by actors and runs them through Yamaha Corporation's Vocaloid software—marketed as "a singer in a box." The result: your voice sounds perfect, making you a synthesized vocalist who sounds far better than even your "singing in the shower" voice.[2] The popularity of the software led to the even greater popularity of fake marketer Hatsune Miku. As part of a brilliant business strategy, the makers of the software envisioned transforming Hatsune from a mere image on a box to a live performance act, demonstrating both the power of the software and the wonder of technological progress.

Their idea worked. Hatsune has become more famous than the product she was originally intended to sell. The 3-D projection of Hatsune Miku performs and prances around several stadium stages a year as part of an international concert tour, where capacity crowds adoringly wave their glow sticks to the rhythm of her music and sing along to the star's chart-topping hit, "The World Is Mine."[3] Female fans come to her concerts wearing outfits, hairstyles, and accessories that mirror their favorite, fraud superstar. She may be only a hologram, but in a world that worships image, and image alone, holograms may have more power than we might suppose.

Just imagine this scene: an arena crowded to capacity with genuine flesh-and-blood people, all there to gaze at an illusion—a technological masterpiece that is as "real" as unicorns or leprechauns. Yet, to the admiring crowd, Hatsune is real. In fact, she is more real than real because she is timelessly picturesque, perfectly on pitch, and masterfully manipulated to appear better than any person ever could.

It is not only imaginary celebrities who experience the power of holograms; now deceased musicians make "live" appearances at concerts to the surprise of their fans. For instance, deceased legendary rap artist Tupac Shakur performed with fellow rappers Snoop Dog and Dr. Dre at the Coachella Music Festival. Rising (or resurrecting) before the awestruck crowd, Tupac performed for thousands of people. Because of the power of holograms, an artist can be frozen in time, replayed whenever the technological puppeteers desire. Cloning the voices and images of belated celebrities is an emerging example of a society that refuses to accept an end to image. Nostalgia and memory has been replaced by nanobytes and memory cards, equipped with the task of making any image or life reproducible until infinity. The ability to reproduce and resurrect images into digital performances subtly teaches us that the real flesh-and-blood life of a star like Tupac is small compared to his image.

We celebrate illusions like Hatsune Miku for what purpose? Why does this hold appeal? Could it be because holograms don't die?

Stranger Than Fiction

The exultation of image, the worship of illusion, and the desire to "veg out" or escape into a technology-guided experience are all subtle attempts to avoid or escape reality.

This leads me to ask: What reality are we escaping from, really?

Why are the lines between real and fake, virtual and material being increasingly blurred, and how come it doesn't seem to bother us much?

Could it be that the reason we adore photoshopped images, technological holograms, and virtual illusions is because they seem eternal, whereas we seem so fleeting and temporary? Does our culture's praise of youth and rejection of the signs of aging unveil a hidden fear that with every new gray hair and every wrinkle death is one step closer?

Woody Allen famously said, "I'm not afraid of death, I just don't want to be there when it happens."[4] Aren't most of us, like Woody, endlessly trying to avoid death, even the topic of death?

Death has always been a whisper in humankind's ears. We try to muffle the whisper with busyness. Our culture is busy discovering new ways to erase wrinkles and extend the shelf life of our hair. It is busy creating potions and lotions that slow aging and perpetuate youth. There is no shortage of empty promises from new pseudoscientific discoveries that assure us if we take this pill, wear this bracelet, or practice this meditation, our life will be extended and thus death delayed. But as much as we talk about the extension of life, at the same time we keep silent about the certainty of death. Death, like politics and religion, has become a taboo topic for most of us.

I have a friend from India who came to America to study at a top university. My friend has observed how sheepish we are in America about death. In India, death is part of the social fabric. Bodies are burned in sacred rivers for anyone to see. Families participate in caring for a loved one's corpse, sometimes for days. Americans, he noticed, experience death as total absence. Americans want to protect themselves from death by making it vanish from their vision quickly. We'd do anything to deny or avoid death altogether.[5] Yet the irony is, until we embrace that we are going to die, we may never actually live.

Our worship of image and youthfulness, our celebration of holograms like Hatsune Miku and other photoshopped fantasies, are subtle attempts to keep the stains of age from us—as far as the East is from the West. Yet to avoid imminent aging and death is to deny our humanity. We must acknowledge that we will indeed die one day. This is part of our story and should inform the vision we have for our lives. Doing so may be the very wake-up call that could liberate us! One of the most basic truths about our humanity is that our life is temporary, and it is from this vantage point that we can begin to rightly think about how we desire to live, and whether or not we are living in a worthy way.

I believe that if most people looked into the mirror of mortality more often, they would have a greater perspective on why they do what they do and whether or not their life is being lived to the full. They would ask deeper and more meaningful questions, and spend more time reflecting on their dreams and the legacy they desire to leave behind.

Sadly, many spend little time thinking about the narrative that forms the story arc of their life. Instead, they are caught up in hours of watching television, surfing the web, or in some cases, trying to cure the disease of death altogether. We avoid death at every turn! We understand death as a problem to solve rather than a certainty to prepare for.

Eternal Images

As a DJ and promoter in rave and club culture for many years, I often witnessed people (including myself) clothed in incredible, flamboyant outfits, with their faces painted in excessive makeup and hair done in entirely unnatural styles. Reality was what we wanted to escape, even if for just a few hours. Image was all that mattered, and every weekend was a competition to see who could look the most dazzling. Everyone looked incredible—angelic even—in fog- and light-filled venues that made up the only community most of us knew. Hundreds of us young and eager club-goers would fill the dance floor of some underground venue and dance in unison for hours until the sun would rise and the music would eventually descend into silence. During those dark, artificially lit hours, enhanced by the mind-bending effects of chemical substances, we felt as one. We were all beautiful, loved, and connected in ways that we believed the world simply did not understand. We were enlightened.

There was a problem though. After hours of moving to the pulsating rhythm of electronic music, the joy would wear off, as would all of the makeup and glamour. Reality would return to us—unwelcome, unbidden, yet inevitable. Behind the fantastic outfits and elaborate makeup were regular people. During most of the week, we did not live up to the image we created for a night of excessive partying. When it came time to evacuate the rave or club in the morning, we would barely look at one another. Under the glow and glitter of lights and laser beams, everyone's image was stunning, yet under the brightness of the morning sun most of us looked like zombies coming back from the dead. Illusion was what most of us wanted, yet the rising sun would reflect reality.

Many of us would daily choose to live in illusion. Our illusions comfort us. They hide from us our true state, protecting us from the truth that terrifies. Losing our illusions is itself a small death. Every time we unweave false reality to uncover the hidden truths of our lives, we assemble a small coffin that holds the now-deceased illusions we once lived by. Burying our illusions is the first step toward resurrecting reality.

The idolization of Hatsune Miku and her technological tribe of counterfeit celebrities simply demonstrates a frightening trend that is becoming more and more prevalent. Image is everything. Substance is being replaced by symbol. Marketing has overrun meaning. Image, however thin and fleeting, wields the power to shape identities. Image is a great beast of our time; much else withers in comparison. In our culture, it is as if the skin of the sacred Scripture has been reshaped to read, "heaven and earth will pass away, yet image will last forever."

The current fascination with virtual reality, including photoshopped pictures of humans airbrushed into "perfect" creatures, paints a startling portrait. We are increasingly bored with ordinary human bodies and the beauty they portray. Pop culture sensation Lady Gaga, renowned for her image-twisting performances and known to refer to her adoring fans as her "little monsters," affirms this startling phenomenon. She writes, "We are nothing without our image. Without our projection. Without the spiritual hologram of who we perceive ourselves to be or rather to become, in the future."[6]

For Lady Gaga, beneath the surface of our image is a boring, dying, and decaying body.

Image, unlike our flesh, does not grow old or fade; it remains the same in its beauty and constant in its perfection. Men and women of all ages do not view images on magazine covers and billboards as caricatures of the human body but rather have subconsciously come to believe that these images are reflective of what people "ought" to look like. Fake has become real.

Do we believe that Lady Gaga is right in saying that image is everything and apart from it we are nothing? I surely hope not. Yet her quip does alarm us into thinking about the daily choices we make between image and reality. What we choose, I suppose, is an unacknowledged feeling that our mirror reflects less than what we view elsewhere. Hope in God has been replaced by a hope in humanity. Our culture has determined that a beautiful human image is something to work for rather than to receive. That we are made in the image of God is a gift that has been left unopened by most. In a godless world, image is master and every person its slave. In a godless world, self-exploration is self-creation. In a world without God and his image-giving love for us, we are left to reinvent ourselves, for ourselves and by ourselves. If we are nothing, and surely headed for nothing, then creating a perfect image is certainly what matters most. This truth has been expressed in pop music as well as in philosophical tomes.

"Men must live and create. Live to the point of tears we must," writes atheist existentialist Albert Camus.[7] The exhausting belief that we are always to make something of ourselves pervades the airwaves and airbrushed images that make up the social landscape of our day. It is not surprising, then, that people exchange identities as often as they buy new wardrobes.

Unfortunately for these folks, self-creation is a myth. None of us create ourselves in a vacuum.

In a time such as ours, when the notion of self-creation reigns supreme, we remain uneasy about who we are and who we ought to become. This anxiety is profitable for those who market self-creation. Of course, self-creation is in direct opposition to what the Bible clearly states, namely that we are made in the image and likeness of God. Sadly, being made in the image and likeness of God matters very little in our time and culture. Being made in the image of a hologram, or Lady Gaga—now, that is worth something!

So sad a display of affectation are the passions of people who desire to be holograms rather than wholly human.

But such is our situation.

Jean Paul Sartre soberly captures the meaning of human life in a world where God is discarded and image is worshiped. He writes, "Every existing thing is born without reason, prolongs itself out of weakness, and dies by chance."[8] If there is no supreme entity telling us who we are or ought to be, our lives are, at the end of the day, unguided occurrences, born out of human will and whim, and have no ultimate reason for being. Sartre would suggest that we are born into a world where God is dead.

We live in a world where many people disregard or deny a belief in God, or at least live in indifference to him. We live in a world perpetually grasping, longing, and searching for something to ground itself as it is tossed to and fro in a raging sea of meaninglessness.

Thus, for Sartre and other culture makers today, for life to have meaning we must make something of ourselves in the brief and fleeting time we have. This is what led Sartre to say, "As far as men go, it is not what they are that interests me, but what they can become."[9]

In Sartre's world, we have no reason for being, no sure and steady way of knowing why we exist rather than not. Yet we do know something with absolute certainty: we are headed for, in Sartre's atheistic view, an eternal darkness of unconscious nothingness.

Plastic People

And so, naturally, as a society, we have become allergic to aging. We are obsessed with youth and glamour, propelling many of us to do everything we can to prevent the aging of our bodies. We seek to erase the signs of time from our faces.

Driven by the desire to look perpetually young, individuals in the United States spent over ten billion dollars on cosmetic surgeries in the year 2010, despite the recession and unstable economy.[10] The fountain of youth is less mythical than it used to be, thanks to Botox and nip and tuck.

Just for a moment, imagine that we still practiced the ancient art of mummification as a society. Picture human corpses treated in such a way that the body would remain intact and the signs of age would be abated instead of being buried six feet deep. Now imagine archaeologists excavating a burial site in Santa Monica or Manhattan five hundred years into the future. As these scientists dig bodies out of tombs and eventually strip away the thick layers of cloth, they'll find silicon implants, plastic noses, and a plethora of augmented appendages instead of simple bones and flesh.

Vanity surely plays a role in our augmentation. Dissatisfaction with one's appearance funds the industries that keep us young. Pointing this out is obvious enough. I want to investigate a layer deeper. What would future cultures conclude about our attitude toward death based on our plastic obsessions? Surely they would conclude that we tried to avoid death at all costs!

Like Hatsune Miku, the adored hologram, we too desire to never age. Hope in technology and submission to its power have created what some call a "post-human" condition. One thinker concludes,

> Perhaps one of the most pressing issues for the twenty-first century will be the impact of new technologies on our experiences and understanding of what it means to be human. For many commentators, this signals the advent of the "post-human condition" in which digital technologies will have the capacity to reconfigure our conceptions of space and time; cybernetic devices will enhance and augment our bodies and minds; and genetic modification will challenge the fixity of "human nature" at its most fundamental level.[11]

Taken to the extreme, some among us believe aging should not be a natural part of life but view aging as a disease to be cured outright.[12] Aubrey de Grey is an eccentric biologist who believes that aging is on its way out. He believes that, in light of the leaps and bounds of technological progress, human life spans will soon increase by mythic proportions. According to

107

de Grey, "Our life expectancy will be in the region of 5,000 years in rich countries in the year 2100."[13] Whether or not such a prophecy will ever come true is not for me to say, even though such a prediction seems rather excessive.

What I do find interesting is that for many, eternal life is no longer a gift from God but rather the potential achievement of human beings. By hook and crook, we will "get out of life alive."[14] Technological progress, as incredible as it is, may be able to extend life, but it cannot reveal to us the purpose of it. Regardless of its genius, technology has not answered the most basic questions humans struggle with. Even if we can extend life by hundreds of years, it does not mean that humans will have a greater sense of why we are alive in the first place. For those who place their faith in such progress, hope in technology, science, and medicine has replaced hope in God. If eternal life is going to be realized, it will surely be through a medical breakthrough rather than divine intervention. Thus, science and technology have become the singular source that millions place their trust in.

Most would gladly pay huge fortunes to acquire the fountain of youth. Is this why we place our hope in the hands of technology, so it can make us into a beautiful image that will live forever?

Sadly, in our culture extension of life has become our only reason for living. Though the desire for life is good, and it is healthy to desire long days, there is a more fundamental anxiety behind our compulsion to live as long as we can. That anxiety is summed up nicely in the pop phrase YOLO, "you only live once."

Death forces us to ask the question, "What are we living for?" rather than "How long will we live?" God, who is eternal, is far more interested in the essence of our lives than the length of them. In fact, if length is the only measure of a person's life, we will steadily lose out on those beautiful witnesses, who by their sacrificial deaths for causes greater than themselves teach us what life is all about to begin with.

When we look death squarely in the face, knowing that life is to be lived more in light of eternity than merely today, we may become free enough to think about the meaning of our life differently. If the meaning of life is only to be the best-looking 112-year-old person, what is the point to living at all?

Meaning and Mortality

We are called by God to "number our days, that we may gain a heart of wisdom."[15] For "all people are like grass, and all their glory is like the flowers of the field; the grass withers and the flowers fall."[16] No matter how self-sufficient and glamorous we become, God "knows how weak we are; he remembers we are only dust."[17] We always stand before God as treasured and deeply loved dust. By embracing this love that God has for us, a love that holds memory of how fragile and fleeting we are, we are liberated from a life of pretension and pretending. Image, like flowers and dust, evaporates in time. All that lasts is the love of God and lives reconciled in the image of their Creator.

Until we peer deep into the well of our own mortality, we will fill our lives with shallow pastimes that make us busy but prevent us from living a life that is rich and meaningful. If we avoid death, we will spend more time focusing on our image rather than our integrity. Steve Jobs, the late CEO of Apple, summed up this point nicely during a speech he gave to a group of graduating students at Stanford:

> No one wants to die. Even people who want to go to heaven don't want to die to get there. And yet death is the destination we all share. No one has ever escaped it. And that is as it should be, because *Death is very likely the single best invention of Life. It is Life's change agent.* It clears out the old to make way for the new. Right now the new is you, but someday not too long from now, you will gradually become the old and be cleared away. Sorry to be so dramatic, but it is quite true.[18]

Death is the great equalizer. It is the only common door that all people from all times and places will walk through. Until we recognize death as a surety and part of our life's story, we will be distracted by the vanities and illusions of this world. We will either be continuously caught up in avoiding our mortality through the pursuits of pleasure or vainly attempt to seek cures for the disease of death altogether. Neither is desirable or possible, for both draw us away from God, who is our only hope in both life and death. Instead, we need to embrace the reality of death, and then, with God's help, we can begin to truly live.

━━━━━

Followers of Jesus must live out a holy refusal to find their identity in image alone. Christians must learn to live in light of eternity. If our world is brought to its knees by the reality of death, then Christians should teach the world to pray while on its knees. For it is true that the darkness of the world leads us to either pretend or pray. Christians must pray rather than pretend. Christians must be people of hope even in the face of death.

We must make true in our world the words of Paul, when he writes,

> Therefore we do not lose heart. Though *outwardly we are wasting away*, yet inwardly we are being renewed day by day. For our light and momentary troubles are achieving for us an eternal glory that far outweighs them all. So we fix our eyes not on what is seen, but on what is unseen, *since what is seen is temporary, but what is unseen is eternal.*[19]

Therefore, we should not hide from, attempt to cure, or deny death. Rather, we should live hopeful and joyful lives as we travel the road of life to its end. We sing and dance and proclaim that God is the God over life and death and it is in him that life is both granted forever and given ultimate meaning. Jesus is and always will be the only resurrection and life. The church must recover peculiar and beautiful practices that prepare us for life with God, both now and forevermore. Part of these practices will surely include hopeful and vibrant worship that equips us to face both death and our eternal, full life with God. At least that is my hope and prayer.

Thomas Merton said it best:

> Our whole life should be a meditation of our last and most important decision: the choice between life and death. We must all die. . . . But the dispositions with which we face death make of our death a choice of either death or of life. If, during our life we have chosen life, then in death we will pass from death to life. . . . If, at the moment of our death, death comes to us as an unwelcome stranger, it will be because Christ also has been to us an unwelcome stranger. For when death comes, Christ comes also, bringing us to everlasting life which He has bought for us by His own death. Those who love true life, therefore, frequently think about their death. Their life is full of a silence that is an anticipated victory over death. Silence, indeed, makes death our servant, and even our friend. Thoughts and prayers that grow up out of the silent thought of death are like trees growing where there is water. They are strong thoughts that have overcome the fear of misfortune because they have overcome passion and desire. They turn the face of our soul, in constant desire, toward the face of Christ.[20]

Questions for Reflection

Why do you think aging has become a disease needing a cure?

What does our culture's obsession with virtual images and photoshopped pictures teach us about our attitudes concerning beauty? Are our attitudes being shaped in helpful or harmful ways?

How does your attitude toward death affect the way you think about what's most important in life?

7

Xeroxed Jesus

I lost myself in Philadelphia.

I had flown to Philly from my home in Orange County to play a series of clubs and raves. It was my first time in the hometown of Rocky and famous Philly cheesesteaks, so I was excited to explore. I was scheduled to DJ three events in three days in some of the most questionable parts of Philadelphia. Raves are illusions in practice, turning some of the most terrifying and run-down sections of a city into an urban wonderland, if only for a night. Founded on the principle of P.L.U.R.—Peace, Love, Unity, and Respect—raves upturn the most horrible and unkempt parts of a city's underground into a living expression of heaven on earth. Well, maybe not quite heaven. On my first night in the city, I was taken by an eccentric club kid named John into the "badlands," an abandoned part of downtown Philadelphia that was home to darkness so thick, police officers neglected the streets.

John was already high on ecstasy, which meant everything he touched reminded him of the first stuffed animal he received as a child; the world was a crib of cuddly wonder.

Whether it was friends' arms, which for him were fleshly passageways into transcendental awe, or his furry and baggy pants, which he stroked obsessively while making a weird motion with his jaw, everything John touched transported him to another world. "It tingles! I'm tingling all over," John repeated to those of us in the car who had not yet dropped ecstasy for the night.

Arriving at a run-down industrial park, I witnessed a concrete jungle transformed into an oasis for partiers. It was around midnight when I began my DJ set. There were about two thousand people crammed into the cold, dilapidated factory, where music ricocheted and sweat dripped to the sound of jungle and house music. My plan was to wait until I finished my set to "E-scape," as we called it then. So when I finished my set around 1:30 in the morning, I decided to drop a pill of ecstasy. After a bit, the drug overtook me. With surreal joy, I began ridiculously groping the cold brick walls that separated the shadowy streets of Philadelphia from the warm flux of movement inside the warehouse. The entire world became a Snuggie.

Enveloped in this chemical fantasy, I distinctly remember having a sudden crisis. I literally forgot who I was. I was overtaken by a fearful amnesia that conquered any sense of clarity or confidence in my identity. I began asking strangers with trembling curiosity, "Do you know who I am? What is my name? Can anyone tell me who I am?"

It wasn't until I saw a few familiar faces who assured me of who I was that I began to recapture my identity. I was so consumed by substances and so captured by a false world that I had lost my grip on reality.

———

My story may be far different from anything you have experienced, but I bet there is at least one similarity. If we took the time to honestly ask ourselves if we have ever felt lost or disconnected from who we truly are, most of us would quietly utter yes. Has there ever been a moment in your life where you felt like your sense of self was under siege? Doesn't it seem at times that people are striving, searching, and sacrificing much to acquire something that will give their life identity and meaning? If people have been overtaken by identity amnesia, how would we know? Or, maybe more provocatively, if the church has forgotten who it is, how would it know? What would be the signs of a church with an identity crisis? Do we live in a time in which the church has lost itself?

I am about to risk a gentle critique of the church that I so deeply love. Proverbs says, "Wounds from a sincere friend are better than many kisses from an enemy."[1] I am a friend and servant of the church because I am a friend and a servant of Jesus.

Yet I must be honest about something. I feel like a perpetual outsider when it comes to many church practices and programs. I have spent the majority of my life dwelling in the secular world, outside the sacred spaces called church. From my vantage point, much of the American church has become married to forms and expressions of entertainment that are at the heart of a self-obsessed culture. Instead of being a powerful witness to an alternative way of life, too many churches have cut out a picture of whatever is trendy in our culture, written the name "Jesus" on it, copied it, and sold a cheap knockoff version of God in the flesh. Have we, in effect, Xeroxed Jesus?

Jesus Christ Superstar

The influence of a culture that is *amusing itself to death* has marched into the sanctuaries of thousands of churches, which then feel compelled to turn the act of worship into a Vegas-like spectacle to amuse the masses. Jesus becomes less Lord and more like "Jesus Christ Superstar." There is a stark difference between being entertained and worshiping. It has little to do with the style of music, lights, or fog machines but ultimately with the call and appeal to give one's life to God. Worship engenders participation and rebukes passivity. Entertainment, on the other hand, does the very opposite. Through entertainment we are trained to watch, not worship. Are our churches creating watchers and consumers instead of worshipers?

Philosopher Hannah Arendt offers a jarring statement that should challenge those enthralled with entertainment religion. We who love the church should heed her words: "There are many great authors of the past who have survived centuries of oblivion and neglect, but it is still an open question whether they will be able to survive an entertaining version of what they have to say."[2]

Arendt's open-ended statement should send a shiver down the spine of anyone interested in the legacy and integrity of the church. It reveals the corrosive ability of turning deep and meaningful subjects into props and comedic clips. If you turn something profound into something entertaining, it loses its inherent value. Maybe it is okay to eventually update something like a Shakespearean play into a version of *The Kardashians*, but can we—or should we—do the same for Jesus? I assume most followers of this radical first-century Jew would answer such a question with a horrified "No!" The raw attraction of Jesus, to most of us who have dared to ditch our life plan and join up with his, is that he is so odd compared to anything we see today. With peculiarity and, at times, offense, Jesus speaks into life a message of enemy love, heavenly charity, and radical peace that is lovely, not laughable.

Much of the church is driven by the need to be relevant to the degree that it has exchanged (or will exchange) worship for performance, sermons for self-help, and community for Christian cabaret. Fearful of being outdated, outdone, or left behind by the world, some churches have adopted strategies and practices that reveal a "whatever it takes" attitude in getting people in the doors and keeping them coming. Or, as one well-known pastor told me in jest, "We will bring an elephant into the sanctuary if it keeps butts in the seats and bucks in the offering." This is a far stretch from Dietrich Bonhoeffer's statement, "When Christ calls a man he bids him come and die."[3]

A. W. Tozer, decades ago, wrote a sober warning that rings true today:

> For centuries the Church stood solidly against every form of worldly entertainment, recognizing it for what it was—a device for wasting time, a refuge from the disturbing voice of conscience, a scheme to divert attention from moral accountability. For this she got herself abused roundly by the sons of the world. But of late she has become tired of the abuse and has given over the struggle. She appears to have decided that if she cannot conquer the great god Entertainment she may as well join forces with him and make whatever use she can of his powers. So today we have the astonishing spectacle of having millions of dollars being poured into the unholy job of providing earthly entertainment for the so-called sons of heaven. Religious entertainment is in many places crowding out the serious things of God. Many churches these days have become little more than poor theaters where fifth rate "producers" peddle their shoddy wares with the full approval of evangelical leaders who can even quote a holy text in defense of their delinquency.[4]

Ouch! Tozer's words sting a bit, don't they? But do they sting without cause, or is there a kernel of truth in the bite of an old theologian?

I think there is. Our only option in reaching our culture is not a "If you can't beat 'em, join 'em" attitude. The gospel is more beautiful than that. Jesus is more eloquent than that. The church is more sacred than that.

Young people are increasingly absent from the church. Statistics pointing to this abound, causing church leaders to ponder why this is so. Many come to the conclusion that we do not have enough "elephants in the sanctuary"; we are not relevant, cool, hip, or edgy enough to reach the entertainment generation. What we need to do, so the reasoning goes, is have more current, louder, and edgier worship services that mimic hot cultural fads. Maybe this means doing a sermon series titled "Real Housewives of the Bible" or inviting a pseudo-celebrity to perform and speak.

Evangelism and church growth become a bait and switch; draw them in with a relevant look and feel and then connect them to the church long-term. There is only one problem: people aren't staying. Among those between the ages of eighteen and thirty, the church is the last place one would go for spiritual insight, let alone entertainment. An additional problem with this approach is that what you catch them *with* is what you attach them *to*. The medium is the message, and if the message is entertainment, you will constantly have people saying things like, "I will go back to church when they have that elephant show again. That was amazing!" It is no wonder that the average attendance for faithful members of any church is twice a month. And those are the faithful members! When church is a form of entertainment, it will also be a peripheral priority instead of an essential and fertile ground for growing deeper into our relationship with Jesus.

Entertainment religion is put into the predicament of offering spiritual goods and services at competitive prices. Churches in local communities end up (unintentionally) switching out members who are looking for a better production. Instead of working at a far-reaching, kingdom-seeking mission to save the lost and heal the least, churches battle over the few believers who actually live in their communities. Whichever church has the best entertainment typically draws the biggest crowds of religious spectators. This, as you can imagine, becomes exhausting for church leaders.

This last year I had one of those "wake-up call" conversations with a pastor I deeply respect. He called me to chat about his calling, which is Christian code for "I'm thinking about leaving ministry." Upon meeting with me, he told me that he realized to be a "successful" pastor in his city he would have to be a combination comedian, CEO, pop psychologist, and motivational speaker, a mix of gifts that God gives to very few people. Overwhelmed by the consumerist expectations of many in his church and on his board, he had written a generous but somber letter of resignation. I probed him as to whether or not it was just exhaustion, and if he needed to take a sabbatical instead of quit. His response was truthful and humble. "Can you take a sabbatical from a culture? The church has changed, and I just can't keep up!"

My pastor friend is seminary trained, gifted beyond belief, and looks the part of what culture would consider "cool." Yet, even with all of his gifts, looks, and passion for Christ and the church, he resigned because he didn't have it in him to be an entertainer. Do we think his experience is unique? Could this be why seven out of ten pastors say they would leave the ministry if they could find a different job that suits them and pays their bills?[5]

How did this happen to the American church?

The Ship of Theseus

During my undergraduate years, I learned about a philosophical puzzle called the Ship of Theseus. It is one of those mind-bending torture devices college professors use to meddle with the minds of people whose frontal lobes are not yet fully formed. Imagine you have a small wooden ship in your backyard and decide that one day you want to take it apart piece by piece. You love your ship, but you have noticed that it is corroding and decaying and needs a bit of an overhaul. You go about taking it apart, tenderly removing each piece of corroded wood. Your intent is not to tear the ship apart; rather, you decide to restore it by replacing every wooden piece you removed with an aluminum piece of the exact same dimensions. When you start this project, you have a completely wooden ship. And at the end of your restoration, you have a ship completely made of aluminum.

But at each distinct stage of the process, you have a ship that is only one piece different than it was previously. Furthermore, suppose that you decide to use the wooden planks you had removed to build another ship materially identical to the original ship. At the end of that project, you'll have two ships, one aluminum and the other wooden, that each claim to be the Ship of Theseus. They can't both be *the* Ship of Theseus, can they? It would seem that one would have to be the original and the other a copy, but which is which? How would you decide which is genuine and which is a reproduction? Is the real ship the one that is made up of all the original pieces, or is the real ship an idea that merely has to hold the shape of the original?

Identity is not as simple to understand as we tend to think. Asking which ship is authentic causes us to question what we mean by *authentic* or *real*. Does *authentic* mean "to be made up of the original parts," and thus any variation or change would mean that something is inauthentic? Or is *authenticity* merely a word that describes what we believe should be the overall shape, feel, or look of something? For instance, "That performance was an authentic portrayal of Mozart's work."

When you call someone authentic, what do you mean?

Let's assume, for a moment, that worship is a central plank of the wood structure that forms the church. That plank has served the church for two thousand years. Worship is defined as a means of laying oneself down for the glory and praise of God. Worship is God-focused, self-denying, and God-gratifying. Such worship has been a faithful plank of wood that, through lyric and rhythm, has helped Christians understand what it means to be shaped by a different story than the rest of the world. Sacred songs shape a sacred people who are able to utter sincere words of devotion and love.

Now imagine that someone (with good intentions) begins to see the plank of worship as irrelevant and unengaging. So they replace that plank with an aluminum piece of the same size and shape, yet this one is called "entertainment." There are enough similarities between worship and entertainment that most don't notice the switch for a while. Both include music and song, but there is a subtle difference. One requires involvement, whereas the other primarily requires observation. One is active, the other passive. One treats people like instruments in an orchestra of praise, whereas the other treats people as bystanders who are there to applaud and appreciate the worship of those up front. A plank of worship that has secured and strengthened the church for centuries has been replaced with a plank of entertainment.

Imagine culturally current planks replacing, piece by piece, the "wood" of the church. Piece by piece, plank by plank, the shape and look of the church starts to morph. Imagine that every piece has now been replaced. Is it the same church? I believe we are living in a time where the church is being forced to determine whether it is the shape or the parts that make up the bride of Christ. Can the medium constantly shift without affecting the message?

Much of the church has lived as if the medium does nothing to hinder the message. The church can be anything so that it can reach anyone. Some would probably label my questioning of this practice as a lack of care about evangelism or mission. Others may say it is naïve to think that the church will not fit into the culture that it inhabits; isn't the church supposed to be incarnational?

My answer is, of course, yes, the church is called to dwell in local communities and bring the gospel of Jesus through word and deed. The problem is not with incarnation but with cultural capitulation.

Just ponder the incarnation for a moment. Jesus, the Son of God, the Second Person of the Trinity, was wrapped in Jewish flesh. He spoke Aramaic, ate kosher, celebrated Jewish festivals, and lived and traveled among average Jews of his day. For all intents and purposes we can say that Jesus was present and culturally close in many ways to his fellow Jews.

Yet Jesus was also a prophetic, incarnate witness to the corruption of his culture. He spoke openly about the downfalls and weaknesses of his own religious tradition. He gathered a group of common people to follow him and be part of his renewed community. He taught this group that they should be different and distinct. They were the "salt of the earth."[6] Jesus redefined for this community how life should be lived. His life was an involvement with and a critique of his culture.

In relationship to power, for instance, Jesus said,

> You know that the rulers in this world lord it over their people, and officials flaunt their authority over those under them. But among you it will be different. Whoever wants to be a leader among you must be your servant, and whoever wants to be first among you must become your slave. For even the Son of Man came not to be served but to serve others and to give his life as a ransom for many.[7]

The church has shameful moments in its history where the words of Jesus were refused and the influence of worldly politics informed church action. The Crusades are but one such blotch upon our record of faithfulness. Unfortunately more stains smear our reputation.

I am the adoptive father of three beautiful children. My eldest daughter, Semeia, is African American, whereas my twins, Asha and Zion, are half Caucasian and half African, as their biological father is from Sierra Leone. Being the father of three incredible children of a race different than my own has caused me to see the world differently. Black is no longer a color to me. In adopting my children I adopted, in some small way, the struggle of those people who have been described as black. The Civil Rights Movement and its struggle to live out the American credo that all men are created equal stretches throughout time and impacts my paternal love. One of the most difficult realities for me to accept in regards to the Civil Rights Movement was the role played by many churches and clergy. Amidst a culture of vicious racism and horrendous oppression, there were too few courageous Christians who fought against the cultural hatred and ignorance of their time.

Martin Luther King Jr., in his famous letter from the Birmingham jail, wrote candidly about his disappointment in the church's ability to stand against the cultural tide and fight for justice.

> I must honestly reiterate that I have been disappointed with the church. I do not say this as one of those negative critics who can always find something wrong with the church. I say this as a minister of the gospel, who loves the church; who was nurtured in its bosom; who has been sustained by its spiritual blessings and who will remain true to it as long as the cord of life shall lengthen. When I was suddenly catapulted into the leadership of the bus protest in Montgomery, Alabama, a few years ago, I felt we would be supported by the white church. I felt that the white ministers, priests and rabbis of the South would be among our strongest allies. Instead, some have been outright opponents, refusing to understand the freedom movement and misrepresenting its leaders; all too many others have been more cautious than courageous and have remained silent behind the anesthetizing security of stained glass windows.[8]

Was it racism that kept much of the church silent? I'm afraid not. I believe the emotion that silenced those commissioned by God was fear. Fear of standing against their culture. Fear of crying out like Jeremiah. Fear of being misunderstood, marginalized by those in power, and unwelcome at the high tables of culture leaders. The values of a dominant culture so intimidated those who were called to be "citizens of heaven" that they hid behind their stained-glass windows while dogs were unleashed upon people made in the image of God.

We may feel that if we lived during such a time we would refuse to appease our culture's ignorance and would be a stick in the spokes of such a wheel of lies. Yet what makes us feel so confident? Do we, in our daily lives and prophetically, stand in opposition to subversive forces that demean and harm other humans? Or do we long to be relevant to a degree that we are impotent to call into question the harmful effects of a culture built on illusion?

———————

Jesus was creating a community that would not be shaped by the dominant values of any culture but would live in tension with those values. Though the disciples lived in space and time, meaning they shared certain customs known to their culture, Jesus infused in them a new citizenship that awakened new vision and practices that formed their way of life in a world that was once common, yet through Jesus had become strange. This practice, this disruption of space and time, continues today as the Spirit of God enlivens hopeful renewal in the hearts of people across the globe. This renewal draws us out of the limits of our culture while infusing us with vision that allows us to see and operate as people who are part of a global, heavenly, and eternal family that transcends space, time, culture, and geography. It is from this angle alone that we are able to ask questions of our culture. We ask as citizens of heaven who are occupying foreign and temporary territory for the purpose of God, and our questions, as heavenly citizens, are far different than those asked in the thrones of Hollywood and Washington, DC. Our practices as aliens and exiles in the world are unique.

For instance, rather than taking an entertainment-driven, shopping-mall approach to church, where relevance is our aspiration, we should make authenticity our goal. We should be authentically weak, unapologetically Jesus-centered, and humbly open to dialogue with culture. As salt and light, our role in the world is to strengthen and enlighten that which is good in our world, as well as tirelessly seeking for God's will to "be done, on earth as it is in heaven."[9] In doing so we may at times look irrelevant and odd to the world, but beautiful in the eyes of God. What would it look like if the church stopped trying to be relevant and instead worked on being uniquely beautiful?

Henri Nouwen prophesies concerning such a church when he says,

> The leaders of the future will be those who dare to claim their irrelevance in the contemporary world as a divine vocation that allows them to enter into a deep solidarity with the anguish underlying all the glitter of success, and to bring the light of Jesus there.[10]

Ironically, when the church recaptures its imagination and fully lives in its divine commission it will become more relevant, and its relevance will be the eternal relevance of the kingdom of God, for which we were made and purposed.

Questions for Reflection

How has the church exchanged, or not exchanged, worship for entertainment?

What cultural forces do you think most affect the church's approach to worship and ministry?

Does the entertainment approach to ministry taken by many churches create disciples of Jesus?

How can the church be relevant without capitulating to cultural fads?

8

Exchanging the Sacred
for the Profane

Children embody wonder. In their eyes, the world is a playground of possibility, awe, and mystery. Within every tree there is a story, under every blade of grass dwells a hidden world of incalculable beauty, encased in every heart is a wellspring of discovery. The world is a sacred place to children. Inanimate objects are endowed with grandeur and personality. The loss of a small toy or the change in a recognizable landscape is, to a child, a mortal blow, a rocking of their moorings. There is no "little thing" for children.

The minds of children wander with illuminated genius. Adults call this immaturity or naiveté. Today, I refuse to believe that maturity is a worthy goal if it means the denial of wonder. When I was a young child I was sensitive, but even more so I was imaginative, believing the world to be a place worthy of exploration and adoration. Every aspect of life to me was so much more than what met the eye.

In front of my small Southern California townhome was a large, majestic tree that separated the driveway of our home from our neighbors'. It probably wasn't a particularly noteworthy tree, in reality, but from my small perspective the tree was a redwood reaching far into the clouds. On the trunk of the tree were beautiful circular knots. Each knot looked like a miniature door. The lines bent perfectly on each knot, as if each one of them were a distinctly designed entryway into the home of a regal chipmunk family.

My cousin and my brother and I would often knock on the knots in attempts to coax the chipmunks out of their homes. They never did answer our call. I assume chipmunks have better things to do than entertain the whims of children. Regardless, once or twice a week we would knock on the knots and speak softly to the chipmunk families, offering them treats if they would greet us with their presence. They never came out, but still the game went on for years, until one day when the tree was unceremoniously cut down.

The tree had grown so large that its roots were upturning the concrete slabs of our driveway. So one Saturday morning a man I did not know came to my house with a gas-powered chainsaw. I can still smell the stink of it. I watched from my bedroom window as the tree, which was home to families of pleasant chipmunks, was struck down in bits and pieces and removed from the front of my home. I cried as I watched the slow and violent death of our grand tree. In consolation, my mother brought me a plastic bag filled with leaves from the tree as a sort of memorial. It helped a bit, but something magnificent and magical was now gone from my world. With the death of a tree came the slow loss of sacredness.

The Loss of Sacredness

Sacredness reflects the special, or even sacramental, nature or "otherness" of some thing, some time, or some person. Mircea Eliade, a scholar of our time, understands the sacred as the "opposite of the profane."[1] Simply put, that which is not sacred is irrefutably profane. In my childhood home there were two sets of dishes available to us. There were the common dishes used for everyday eating, and then there was the "china," which was reserved for banquets, birthdays, and holiday dinners. One set of dishes was profane, the other sacred.

"Sacred" also means we observe the world with a set of lenses that sees, and expects to see, more than meets the eye. "Profane" means all things are common. There is nothing more than what is easily noticeable. The loss of sacredness happens when more and more of your world goes from being special, wondrous, and unique to being just commonplace, ordinary, and dull.

The word *just* commonly accompanies the loss of the sacred. It is "just" a tree, "just" sex, "just" my body, "just" fun, "just" church, "just" God, "just . . ." What a terrible word, *just*. I am committed to removing it from my vocabulary. When something is reduced to "just" a thing, it is pillaged of wonder and the slow loss of sacredness begins.

Can you remember any moments when this happened for you? Was it when you discovered there actually wasn't a Santa Claus? Christmas became a little more ordinary after that for a lot of us. Did sacredness die along with your parents' marriage? Daily life became a little more isolated and lonely after that, didn't it? Can you mark the moments where the magic was whisked out of your world? When did "reality" kick in for you?

In the words of Sigmund Freud, "Illusions commend themselves to us because they save us pain and allow us to enjoy pleasure instead."[2] For Freud, children live in a dense haze of deception that thaws in adulthood. The natural progression is from illusion to reality, from sacred to sensible. And, of course, part of this growing up in the world is discarding God. Freud sees God as the foundational myth that keeps the human species in adolescence. As he writes, "Religion is an illusion and it derives its strength from the fact that it falls in with our instinctual desires."[3]

What Freud implies is that religion, those institutions that thrive on their belief in God or the supernatural, are constructed perfectly to give us what we most desire. The only problem for Freud is that what we most desire is a lie. Religion and its fictional counterparts are residues of our infancy. They neither reveal truth about the world nor liberate human beings to achieve their fullest. They are shackles upon the mind and heart of progress.

Freud's opinion is certainly not unique. He is only one of many thinkers who share a long and complex history of skepticism, which has had as its goal the disenchantment of the world of wonder, making it mundanely accessible to human reason. Max Weber, one of the founders of sociology, wrote many years ago, "The fate of our times is characterized by rationalization and intellectualization and, above all, by the disenchantment of the world."[4]

What he meant is that our times are founded on the assumption that everything we touch, smell, taste, and experience can be reduced to human understanding. This is called science. Trees are trees. Humans are animals. Life is biological. Our origins are random. And the story goes on and on. All other claims to knowledge fall in the realm of "feeling" and are dismissed as the ramblings of unsophisticated newcomers to the world of reason. The so-called New Atheists, the more popular being Richard Dawkins, Sam Harris, Daniel Dennett, and the late Christopher Hitchens, have sold millions of books founded on this simple assumption of secularization.

Charles Taylor, one of the most esteemed thinkers of our time, has written much on the triumphant march of secularization, noting its implications for our era. In his book *A Secular Age*, he asks, "Why was it virtually impossible not to believe in God in, say, 1500 in our Western society, while in 2000 many of us find this not only easy, but even inescapable?"[5] Ponder this sentence for a moment. In five hundred years or so, the preeminent beliefs about God have moved from natural to suspect, from important to petty, from essential to peripheral. How did this massive shift in thinking happen?

Taylor understands the centrality of God in the minds of others today to have retreated in a few crucial ways. On the whole, people no longer see natural events as acts of God. Some people still view hurricanes as God's judgment and earthquakes as outbursts of God's wrath, but if they express that publicly, they will quickly bear the brunt of criticism and ridicule. Although these bold statements are most often expressed in ways that are premature, offensive, and short-sighted, the underlying assumption that God would play a part in natural cataclysmic events is clearly seen as prehistoric thinking. The natural world is commonly seen now as something separate from the realm of God's creative love and intimate interaction.

Many people who do believe in God believe in a deist God who ignited the Big Bang, spun the Earth on its axis, and then went on vacation—what well-known sociologist Christian Smith calls "moralistic theistic deism." By this he means that modern people believe God is responsible for our moral compass, that some force like God does exist though who or what it is is foggy, and that this force of some kind is not currently involved in our world. In other words, God is a force out there who spun the world on its axis, backed away once it began to turn, and wants us to be nice to one another. Anything else said of or believed about God tends toward "fundamentalism" or "mythology."

Some modern-day apologists, defenders of the Christian faith, thrive on proving the existence of this sort of God. Debates with atheists abound trying to convince them of a first cause, a prime mover, a cosmic initiator who commands belief and obedience. One wonders whether this is the God whom Christians for thousands of years have referred to as triune. Needless to say, God's daily interaction with the world is seen as increasingly suspicious, and for some, the stuff of ancient fairy tales.

I wish I could say that only secular, atheist thinkers hold this opinion, but even some devout evangelicals seem to share a similar view. The movement from belief in a God who works "in the world" to belief in a God who lives "in my heart," guiding personal moral decisions, may be a sign that we no longer believe God is at work in the world in the ways the Bible seems to profess.

Secularization includes more than the general decline of religious belief and practice in our world. In questioning belief in God, a judgment is also cast upon those of us who profess such a belief. God is not the only one held in suspicion; humans are as well. Both believers and unbelievers become suspect when God dies in the human psyche. Thus the corresponding activity of religious practices and communities are understood by a growing number to be throwbacks to an ancient way of life for less-evolved humans. The so-called death of the mainline church, and the growing disinterest in organized religion, is a mere outgrowth of secularization.

Skepticism inherent in our culture has led to withdrawal from organizations built on assurance. Only doubt is sure. This is the grim atmosphere in which believers believe and practice their faith. We have been convinced that belief is a private matter. Religion is like someone's personal taste in ice cream. It is just a matter of preference. We all know tastes tell us little about the world versus the person. What sense does it make to argue in the public arena whether rocky road is superior to chocolate chip?

And Religion Is . . . ?

Religion is a very difficult word to define in its own right. Think about it: How would you define religion? Is it simply belief in God? William Cavanaugh, a Roman Catholic scholar, has written that *religion* has "nothing close to agreement among scholars."[6] He goes on to state that, "there is a significant and growing body of scholars . . . who have been exploring the ways that the very category religion has been constructed in different times and different places. . . . Religion is a constructed category, not a neutral descriptor of a reality that is simply out there in the world."[7] According to Cavanaugh and a growing number of thinkers, "religion is not simply found, but invented. The term religion has been used in different times and places by different people according to different interests."[8]

So if Cavanaugh is correct, and I think he is, why are there new "anti-religious" movements in the United States when the term is nearly impossible to define? Why is "religion" the punch line of famous comedians like George Carlin and Ricky Gervais? The word *religion* is derived from the Latin word that means "to bind," or "to hold together." Thus I am led to believe that what most people criticize when they launch an attack on religion are the forces it has displayed in "binding" people together.

In Christianity's case, what are the forces that have bound people together? Certainly there has been the social and political power of the church throughout the ages. That the church has at times been co-opted by forces, or itself has been a force for evil in the world, is a given. Even disciples and churches unfortunately find the pull of the world and its means of dealing with power attractive. Maybe what people mean when they say they are "spiritual and not religious" is that they do not want to be associated with those people who are thought to have launched the Crusades, have blown up abortion clinics, and who hate gay people. If these things were or are the soul of Christianity, I myself would be in agreement with the exodus from religious to spiritual. When Christianity attempts to establish its truthfulness with the sword or the spear, it has ceased to be Christianity.

Could it be that what most critique as sickly or disregard as fantasy in Christianity is not Christianity at all? Could what Danish Philosopher Søren Kierkegaard wrote many years ago be still true today, namely that "Christendom has done away with Christianity without being quite aware of it"?[9]

Though the institutions and perversions of Christianity are fodder for comedians and critics alike, does our longing for sacredness still make room for a fresh work of God in our world? Though secularism has increased with force, there still remains a popular belief in God and a deep desire for spirituality. People still long for more. Atheism, though growing, is still a small slice of the spiritual landscape. And for many the reductionist picture of human life offered by atheists such as Dawkins and Hitchens just does not seem to add up to the sense of wonder and spirituality they experience on a daily basis. Though for hundreds of years people have declared the slow death of religious institutions, God, and spirituality, all three remain. The human spirit still hungers for more than bread alone.

C. S. Lewis wrote what I find to be a very profound assessment of our spiritual starvation:

> Creatures are not born with desires unless satisfaction for these desires exists. A baby feels hunger; well, there is such a thing as food. A duckling wants to swim; well, there is such a thing as water. Men feel sexual desire; well, there is such a thing as sex. If I find in myself a desire which no experience in this world can satisfy, the most probable explanation is that I was made for another world.[10]

Our lives are built for wonder and sacredness. We are not "just" creatures, we are image bearers who have an inbuilt homing mechanism leading us back to the "otherness" that is God. Some deny this. Others pollute it. And still others open their entire lives to it.

What about you? What does your heart tell you?

————

For most of my life I would have classified myself as "spiritual not religious." Confused about God, I said I believed in him as a way to end conversations with aggressive evangelists. Deep down I knew little about God, though I lived most of my life with a deep sense of spiritual longing. I have been forever haunted by the sacred, and since I was a small child I longed for it. In my young adult years, I attempted to experience the sacred through music and art and drugs and sex, and at times I felt as if I had grasped the pinky finger of the sacred but never fully held its hand. I sensed a voice speaking inside of me, saying, *Where are you?*

I want more of you.

There is more to life than this.

This sacred voice, "speaking" to me, was one I could not recognize. But I owed it a response; this persistent and loving voice was moving my soul closer to the source of Truth.

The presence of God haunts the human imagination. Even in the hearts and minds of those who consider him dead, his voice still invokes a sacred echo. Wonder whispers at us all. Among the silence dwells the sacred. Or, in the words of Mircea Eliade, "To whatever degree he may have desacralized the world, the man who has made his choice in favor of a profane life never succeeds in completely doing away with religious behavior."[11]

Our longing for sacredness exists, and like a starving person willing to eat anything to satiate his hunger, many of us have turned toward trivial objects and practices in our religion. We can't escape being religious; we just replace the object of our religion.

Replacement Religion

A phrase attributed to G. K. Chesterton goes, "When a man stops believing in God he doesn't then believe in nothing, he believes anything."[12] With the eclipse of traditional belief in God comes a long line of unworthy idols who clamor for our attention. Our obsession with the lives of celebrities, television shows, movies, music, and video games has become for us a replacement religion. No longer merely hobbies or playthings, they claim to offer us meaning and purpose.

Similarly, money has also become an unworthy idol. Is money just a tool for life, or has it become the goal of life? Eternal security is no longer faith in Jesus but rather a life insurance policy and a 401(k) account. Or think about our obsession with youthfulness and beauty. We desire to be forever young and keep the sting and signs of death far from us. Instead of depending on God for our joy, meaning, purpose, and significance, we spend years in trivial pursuits that leave us parched and hollow. And the result is not that we become atheists; rather, we become idolaters and end up believing in anything, just as Chesterton predicted.

The irony of our time is that though we are supposed to be more skeptical, scientific, and calculating than any of our forebears, many of us are remarkably fascinated by and believe in everything from telepathy to poltergeists to haunted houses to ancient aliens to UFOs to horoscopes to astrology to crystal healing to pop-culture psychics. These fascinations are found and followed on reality TV shows, popular websites, magazines, and movies.

From *Long Island Medium* to *Celebrity Ghost Stories*, our culture is obsessed with profane expressions of the sacred. These popular shows reveal a new religious landscape of movements that are on the rise. It is estimated that "perhaps 1,000 to 2,000 new religious movements have arisen in the United States alone in the twentieth century, and few of these are rooted in traditional Judeo-Christian theological assumptions."[13] Where there is a religious hunger among the people, there will be cheap ways to satisfy it. The longing for sacredness remains, and the impulse endures. Our desire for God, for sacredness, for something beyond our senses, for that which requires imagination is not merely a childish longing or a carryover from a less sophisticated time. It is inescapably human and gracefully divine.

What would it be like if the church were a cultivator of the sacred in a profane world?

Questions for Reflection

Think of a time in your life when you lived with a sense of sacredness. What was going on in that moment that made you feel like life was more than meets the eye?

Do you remember a time in life when you experienced a loss of the sacred? What happened and how did it affect your view of the world?

How does your belief or disbelief in God affect the way you see the sacredness of life?

What are some signs of our culture's longing for sacredness?

Part 2

THE PURSUIT
OF WHOLENESS

9

Bringing Sacred Back

Jesus *is* and *was* earthy. His stories and metaphors were not those of the graphic spectacle of ancient entertainment such as those of the Greek gymnasium or theatre, or even the popular Roman games. Instead he talked about seeds and soil, sheep and goats. He was earthy because to be fully human is to be from the earth. Like every seed, we too began in the ground. *Adam* in Hebrew means "out of the dirt" or "dirt man." As well-dressed as we may be, God remembers that we are dust and not much more, for from "dust we came and to dust we shall return."[1]

The world that God created and pronounced as good is a world populated with dirt particles, gnats, and thorn bushes. Jesus was God's offering to this sacred yet profaned world, this world intended to be good yet bent toward vulgarity. This world that was supposed to be singular and sacred has become two worlds, really, the sacred and the secular. As we have already noted, these mix like oil and vinegar. Religion and secularism duel for predominance in this neatly barricaded universe of ours.

God, on the other hand, seems to have intended the world to exist as a sacred space that would form fully integrated individuals. The garden we refer to as Eden derives from the Hebrew word for *harmony*. *Sacred* would be appropriate as well. Yet we are accustomed to using words like *natural* and *supernatural*. The sacred belongs to the supernatural view. Natural refers to the home of humanity, whereas supernatural refers to the home of God.

Even for many believers, this is how the world operates. There are two tiers to life. There is "up there" where God reigns in glory, surrounded by choirs of angels and fog machines no doubt, and "down here," where glory is washed away through natural suffering, pain, and predictable processes. A miracle, in this view, is a breaking into the natural order, a sacred stitch in time. Most of life is left to normative routines such as the sun rising in the morning or gravity clutching all things in its mighty grip. Yet such a view is not in line with the Christian tradition. The sacred is both natural and supernatural. Sacredness is earthy as well as celestial. The Bible says that the totality of the universe belongs to God. Our lives here and now are not detached from the handiwork of a creative, loving God. To be human is to be divine in the sense that we are formed, fashioned, and designed to function as an image of the Creator.

We cannot escape our sacredness, we can only pervert it. The incarnation, the event in which God became embodied in space and time, was the moment that God put on the perishable, earthy, and vulnerable flesh of humanity to reaffirm it and the world as sacred spaces. God came in Jesus and planted a flag of victory deep into the land of occupied territory, reclaiming it as property of his kingdom. You are land as well. Every breath and beat of your heart, every sound-filled second and every still moment of silence, all relationships and recreations, all homes and hospitals, every heart and mind are soil for the sacred.

Some will ask, "What about all the darkness and evil in the world? Are they home to the sacred as well?" to which I would, of course, answer no. But they are, interestingly enough, signposts to the sacred. Saint Augustine offers what I believe to be the most profound understanding of evil for the very reason that he understands it as the loss of some good, or sacredness, rather than a gloomy monster hidden in the closet. We must again remember, as Augustine did, that God created the world and it was perfect, without any evil or suffering. Sacredness was everywhere. As we read in the Bible, "God saw all that he had made, and it was very good."[2]

Augustine understood evil as the privation of goodness. Evil is the loss or deprivation of goodness, just as blindness is a loss of sight. Evil is the gap where good should be. Evil originates when we refuse God and settle for a lesser form of goodness, creating loss of goodness, as the narrative of the fall in Genesis 3 teaches so well. The fall is not the total destruction of the good world God created; rather it is the perversion and profaning of God's world. The story of redemption is a reminder of the sacredness of life.

Do we "have eyes to see and ears to hear?" If what I am proclaiming to you is true, what is the responsibility of the people of God in "bringing sacred back"? How can the church help people "hear" and "see"? We need to reclaim that which is sacred in our spaces, our people, and our stories.

Sacred Spaces

Has there ever been a place that overflowed with significance for you? Just being there caused your heart to flutter. Whatever this place was, whether a building, a home, or a vacant lot that contains a library of memories, some spaces have the ability to rekindle feelings and beliefs that we have forgotten along the way. Though the world shines with sacredness, a dark shroud conceals from us the innate beauty and divinity sustaining and forming all things. Therefore we need certain places, times, people, and rhythms that remind us of the sacredness of which we were created to partake. In the Christian tradition, *pilgrimage* is the word used to describe the journey to sacred spaces. These special places are where the veil between heaven and earth is most transparent.

If the church is to recover our role as cultivators of the sacred, we must learn to view the place of our gathering as a body of believers as sacred space. Place matters. I fear the viral nature of our connected world displaces us from recognizing that holy ground still exists.

God, from the earliest chapters of the Bible, sets apart gardens and tents and temples as spaces that pointed to his presence and purpose for the world. How we gather and where we gather matters. Material life is central to the worship of God. Unlike those who highlight mission alone as the central category of the church, I believe the church has to recover the idea that worship of God is in some sense the sanctifying, or making holy, of certain places. Yes, the church is the people, not the building. I'm not arguing against the idea that we are the temple of the Holy Spirit. But as living temples, it would be silly for us to underestimate the roles space and location have in spirituality. Place determines posture, and to a large extent the spaces in which we dwell condition us to view the world uniquely.

In a world where community is mediated through tablets and phones, and money is transmitted digitally, the church must locally embody a sacred existence in physical form. The church should be lived in a space that embodies sacredness in creative and physical ways. The term *sanctuary* has become passé in most growing evangelical churches, being replaced by terms of utility like *auditorium*. The sanctuary, however, was the place set aside to remind those within its walls that the world is sacred. We are sacred people on a sacred journey, and thus gather in sanctuaries.

So what constitutes a sacred space? It is a physical environment that is reserved for worship and communion with

God. Yes, this can be anywhere, but I fear that if "anywhere" is the only descriptor of the place we operate with special focus on God, we in the end easily avoid him everywhere. A sacred space is not more special than others in itself; rather, it is made special because of the unique attentiveness you have before God there. Churches should be sacred spaces rather than just auditoriums, because it is within them that the rule of heaven is proclaimed over the lives of disciples. Thus the space is made sacred because those there are going to meet God there.

If one can become so spiritual that the entire world is an altar before God, then surely my precaution here matters little. I would say, though, that those in the great tradition of Christian spirituality who have arrived at such a place have done so because at one time they reserved spaces in their world for reflection and worship. Eventually those spaces became bigger until their whole world became the throne of God. Yet most of us, myself included, need to start somewhere to gain such revelation. My hope is that church would be that place for us.

How does the physical space where our churches meet inspire people to see and participate in the sacred?

How does the rhythm of weekly worship in a certain physical space cultivate hearts and minds to see the world as created and redeemed by God?

Do the spaces that house our worship help or hinder people in viewing the sacredness of the world?

If we are to bring back the sacred, we must cultivate sacred spaces that stimulate the knowledge of the sacredness within us. We must heed the words of God to Moses: to stand in God's presence is to stand on holy ground.

Sacred People

In a world that is increasingly critical toward religion, the church must recover the notion of forming sacred people as

145

a way of answering the world's skepticism. In other words, the church has to begin looking at what it does as larger than merely "saving" people. We must return to the business of becoming *sanctified* people.

The Bible describes those who are sanctified as "saints." Most people when hearing the word *saint* immediately think of "Holy Rollers," arrogant religious types who self-proclaim their sainthood, or Mother Teresa types who seem to have something that very few other people in the world actually have. Most people, when asked if they are a saint, would giggle and say, "No, not me!" Yet the New Testament writers often referred to those who had been redeemed by Christ as "saints." Thomas Merton remarked, "A saint is not someone who is good but who has experienced the goodness of God."[3]

What gives the gospel credibility and the church its power is the embodiment of sacredness that changes human hearts and lives. Human beings are God's project and therefore are conduits of his presence and power. We carry his glorious treasure in our clay pots, and by carrying his glory we are thus glorified. Humility and awe are the only responses appropriate for a saint. A saint is more attuned to their own sinfulness and need, thus they are committed to Jesus as the only source of their sacredness. Saints are people who view individuals in light of God's love for them. People matter—they are not only *matter*. Thus saints are driven by a sacred vision that works for justice, equality, redemption, and healing, for these are attributes that flow from the sacred.

To view people through the lens of sacredness is to view people as whole. They are more than component parts such as their income, youthful looks, intellect, charisma, or abilities. They are lightning rods buried into the soil of God's good world who are constantly struck by the wonder and touch of God. We should approach saints with awe, for they—for we—are living sanctuaries, altars in the world. In a galaxy where celebrities are the brightest stars, saints should be supernovas, blinding the false icons of our time. Sacred people are informed by sacred stories. We are characters in a magnificent plot of creation, fall, and redemption.

It has been said that our potential is largely based on the stories we accept as true about ourselves and the world. In the next chapter we will look at the role of the Bible in giving depth to our sacred journey, as well as providing the script that will shape our lives with meaning and purpose. You play a role in this sacred story.

Questions for Reflection

Do you currently have a place that is a significant space you go to for spiritual experiences? Where is it?

Does your average church experience create a sense of sacredness in you? If so, what elements do this? If not, what other feeling does it create instead?

How can the church act in ways that spark the imagination of people to once again discover God in their midst?

10

Bringing Scripture Back

The Bible is famous. It is the most talked about, written about, argued about, and misunderstood book in the world. It is the only book that I know of that has birthed its own primetime TV game show, *The American Bible Challenge*, hosted by acclaimed "redneck" comedian Jeff Foxworthy. Contestants are quizzed on their knowledge of biblical stories, characters, verses, and theological principles, winning prize money for every correct answer. It is a good Christian show, of course, in that the contestants play for fun and give the winnings to charity. This TV show is on a secular network, is sponsored by secular corporations, and is viewed by tens of thousands of people of diverse spiritual opinions and backgrounds. How is it that a collection of ancient documents commands the attention of so many?

The Bible is revered by billions of people. Bibles can be found in most hotel rooms. Presidents and other political figures are sworn into office in a ceremony that requires them to place their hand on a Bible. Before testifying in a court of law, the Bible is evoked as a sign that what one will say is a matter of absolute truth. There are more copies printed of the Bible in a given year than all other top-selling books combined. Yet, although the Bible is virtually everywhere and is the bestselling book of all time, many do not know its contents or live their lives by it.

For years, "Evangelical pollsters have lamented . . . the disparity between Americans' veneration of the Bible and their understanding of it, painting a picture of a nation that believes God has spoken in Scripture but can't be bothered to listen to what God has to say."[1] Millions have come to the conviction that believing the Bible is holy is a good thing, but beyond that tepid declaration of belief, the Book's principles and truths are largely ignored. It appears that believing in something as an act of faith is far more important than knowing the content of that faith.

Professor Stephen Prothero, a Harvard-educated scholar of American religion, has written much on biblical illiteracy in America. In his bestselling book *Religious Literacy: What Every American Needs to Know and Why*, he writes, "Biblical illiteracy has been fairly well documented. In fact, according to the Gallup Organization, which has tracked trends in US religion for over fifty years, Bible reading has declined since the 1980s and 'basic Bible knowledge is at a record low.'"[2] He continues:

> Virtually every American home has at least one Bible, publishers sell about twenty million Bibles annually, and Gideons International gives away a new Bible every second of every day. Moreover, nearly two-thirds of Americans believe that the Bible holds the answers to all or most of life's basic questions, and a majority claims that it reads that book at least twice a month. If so, Americans are not reading particularly carefully.[3]

Once again we observe that believing in the Bible is far more common than knowing the sacred Scriptures. There have been many studies done on the average American's understanding of basic Bible facts, and the results are disheartening. When it comes to knowing the Bible, apart from a few hotshot game show contestants, Americans flunk out in terms of biblical literacy. For instance,

- Only half of American adults can name even one of the four Gospels.
- Most Americans cannot name the first book of the Bible.
- Only one-third know that Jesus (no, not Billy Graham) delivered the Sermon on the Mount.
- A majority of Americans wrongly believe that the Bible says that Jesus was born in Jerusalem.
- When asked whether the New Testament book of Acts is in the Old Testament, one-quarter of Americans say yes. More than a third say that they don't know.
- Most Americans don't know that Jonah is a book in the Bible.
- Ten percent of Americans believe that Joan of Arc was Noah's wife.[4]

Some of these misunderstandings are admittedly funny, but they are also shocking. Personally, the most alarming issue I have with the growing biblical illiteracy is the internal contradiction it illuminates. Millions of people who are supposedly basing their entire life and eternity upon the content of this book, believing it offers intimate details about life and how it ought to be lived, admit in the same breath they lack thorough knowledge of it. When asked in a survey if they believe the Bible is the word of God, most would give an affirmative and impassioned yes. But when quizzed on some of the most obvious points of Scripture, belief turns into confusion. Nevertheless, for many this does not seem cause for alarm. What matters to most, and what seems to be given much more street cred, is the amount of faith you have, not the amount of knowledge you have.

The disparity of living in this way can be seen in applying this same mind-set to relationships, especially marriage.

Could you honestly say you shared intimacy with your husband or wife if you couldn't describe their taste in food or recall the name of their hometown?

"I may not know their middle name, but I have faith that they have one and that is enough."

When you love someone, it follows that you want to know the most intimate details concerning them. Incidentals are important when intimacy is at play, aren't they? Yet for millions of Christians, the Bible is believed in and not known. They ring the Bible bell to argue against abortion or homosexual marriage, but when asked to offer a passage that justifies their condemnation many come up empty-handed. This, of course, further cements the public persona of Christians in the eyes of the media, namely that we are Bible thumpers, not Bible students. Some go so far as to call the Bible inerrant and perfect, yet their "perfect" book collects dust in their hearts and minds. How can so many people supposedly believe in and revere the Bible but not know or script their lives according to it?

We must recover the Scriptures as the central soul-shaping medium through which we can discern truth from fiction and transcendent beauty from triviality. It is essential that we ground our lives in the truths of God as found in the Bible. We cannot understand God's purpose for us and live with substance and depth if we believe in, but largely ignore, the sacred Scriptures.

Biblical illiteracy means followers of Jesus will lose the plot of God's evolving story and become more captive to the *trivial*. Other narratives and scripts will grab hold of our hearts, and over time the Bible will become ancillary to finding meaning and purpose. One of the central ways we exit out of the trivial is by entering into the richness God desires for us through the living, breathing Word of God. The Scriptures teach us the difference between reality and fiction, between imagination and idols, and ultimately about the one true God. Using Scripture to narrate our lives can reeducate, re-form, and deepen individuals and communities alike, so we can embrace the beautiful and complex reality of God's creative will, of which we are a part.

Schizophrenic Stories

The 2001 film *A Beautiful Mind* is a compelling movie that reveals the remarkable power of narrative to bring harm or healing to a human life. John Nash is an awkward but brilliant student at Princeton University who has a promising future in the field of mathematics. Nash goes to college, meets a charismatic roommate studying literature, and makes his way into all that goes along with college life. Eventually he is invited by the Pentagon to crack enemy communications for the United States government. Because of his mathematical genius, Nash is able to decipher cryptic codes completely in his head. He becomes enthralled with his new occupation.

Nash begins to work for the United States Department of Defense, where his job is to look for cryptic patterns in magazines and newspapers in order to detect encoded Soviet communications related to activities on American soil. He becomes increasingly obsessive about searching for these hidden patterns, and believes he is being watched and followed when he delivers the results of his work to a secret government mailbox. His anxiety increases as he sees more and more patterns of a Soviet takeover everywhere. The story he lives in is suffocating. His world is consumed by secret signs and hidden enemies. Nash is brilliant but alone, and gradually the audience starts to understand that Nash's story is actually a lie.

Nash is a schizophrenic who lives in an illusory universe of concealed threats and undisclosed puzzles. Even his beloved and trusted roommate is fictitious. Of course, when confronted with his disease and the compulsive behavior that flows from it, Nash suspects it all to be part of a secret plot determined to silence the one person who understands what is really going on behind the curtain. He thinks he sees the world as it really is, and only over time does he begin to shift his acceptance from one narrative to another. He has to begin to evaluate the story that structured his life, discerning truth from fiction. His survival is dependent upon learning to narrate the world accurately.

I want to suggest that what is true for Nash is also true for us. None of us (including me) sees the world as it is, because we are prone to live under deceptive narratives. And I've been talking about some of the dominant narratives that form our lives in hopes of exposing their futility and inability to appease the cravings of our souls. Whether we like it or not, all of us live our lives to the rhythm of someone else's drum. Individualism is largely a myth. Whether we are obsessed with wealth or beauty or we outsource our brains to technology, none of us is free from living within a story that structures our lives. This ought not cause us to feel shame or guilt, but rather humility and caution.

━━ ━━ ━━

In the words of the apostle Paul, we "see things imperfectly, like puzzling reflections in a mirror, but then we will see everything with perfect clarity."[5] His words flow directly out of his experience as a Pharisee who was convinced that he knew who God was and how he acted. He is a perfect example of someone who had the truth of his narrative confronted and changed. Paul was a violent persecutor of the church who oversaw the death of one of the earliest proclaimers of the gospel, Stephen. The book of Acts records the transformation of Saul the persecutor into Paul the apostle. We read in Acts 9,

> Meanwhile, Saul was still breathing out murderous threats against the Lord's disciples. He went to the high priest and asked him for letters to the synagogues in Damascus, so that if he found any there who belonged to the Way, whether men or women, he might take them as prisoners to Jerusalem. As he neared Damascus on his journey, suddenly a light from

heaven flashed around him. He fell to the ground and heard a voice say to him, "Saul, Saul, why do you persecute me?"

"Who are you, Lord?" Saul asked.

"I am Jesus, whom you are persecuting," he replied. "Now get up and go into the city, and you will be told what you must do."

The men traveling with Saul stood there speechless; they heard the sound but did not see anyone. Saul got up from the ground, but when he opened his eyes he could see nothing. So they led him by the hand into Damascus. For three days he was blind, and did not eat or drink anything.[6]

I find it fascinating that Paul's encounter with Jesus blinded him. Have you ever thought about this? How does the "light of the world" cause someone to become blind? Could it be Paul was struck blind as a way to reveal his spiritual blindness? Saul the persecutor was blind to the story of God's salvation and therefore he needed to undergo physical blindness so that his eyes could be opened afresh by an experience of the living Jesus. In other words, Jesus blinded Paul so he could ultimately make him see the world as it really is.

Whether we like it or not, all of us are like Paul in some way. We are born into the world with a foggy set of lenses over our eyes. Therefore we are prone to seeing the world dimly and need aid to see the world as it really is. All have eyes, but not all eyes see. The Bible ought to be the source from which we script our lives.

Living by the Right Script

The Bible is not without its complexity, and we must acknowledge that we cannot know God to the degree that he knows himself. However, Christians throughout history have believed that the Bible is integral to being in relationship with God and experiencing the abundant life he has for us. I take the view held by many classical theologians that the Bible is a form of revelation; meaning it is one of the ways God has disclosed part of his person and purpose to the world.

As Karl Barth wrote, "The statement that the Bible is God's Word is a confession of faith, a statement of the faith which hears God himself speak through the biblical word of man."[7] The Bible contains the Word of God and retains power when read as such. Therefore I take issue with historicists who splice and dice the Bible into bits and pieces, removing the possibility that the Bible speaks with a unified voice.

Philosopher Søren Kierkegaard lived in a time when scholars were reducing the Bible from sacred text to historical document. Disturbed, Kierkegaard wrote,

> The matter is quite simple. The Bible is very easy to understand. But we Christians are a bunch of scheming swindlers. We pretend to be unable to understand it because we know very well that the minute we understand, we are obliged to act accordingly. Take any words in the New Testament and forget everything except pledging yourself to act accordingly. My God, you will say, if I do that my whole life will be ruined. How would I ever get on in the world? Herein lies the real place of Christian scholarship. Christian scholarship is the Church's prodigious invention to defend itself against the Bible, to ensure that we can continue to be good Christians without the Bible coming too close. Oh, priceless scholarship, what would we do without you? Dreadful it is to fall into the hands of the living God. Yes it is even dreadful to be alone with the New Testament.[8]

For Kierkegaard, the Scripture is plain enough for us to obey it. The problem is not in our understanding but in our obedience. Skeptical scholarship has made the message of Jesus much more complicated than it needs to be. For centuries the primary approach to biblical studies has been solely historically oriented. The "who," "what," and "where" questions have had two unfortunate outcomes. On one hand are those who endeavor to treat the Bible merely as a historical document. They come to find a troubled history of interpretive skepticism as to what we can really know about the past. This skepticism, when applied to Jesus, has the unfortunate outcome of creating a minimalistic ghostlike persona who is impotent when compared to the robust Jesus known through a more "naïve" reading of the Gospels and trust in the work of God through his Word and Spirit. On the other hand are those who, through history, come to find a Jesus who is rich and full of color. They find his magnificence only grows through placing him in his historical context. Yet the immediate presence of God as expressed in the Gospels subtly feels more about "then" than "now," and their experience of God becomes lessened by the comparison to the "good old days."

Kierkegaard is fighting both of these forms of "historicism," which root the spiritual quest so far in the ancient past that they neglect the immediate and pressing question, "What is God saying now?" Or, maybe an even better question, "What is God requiring of me in this very moment?" Unless we believe the Bible is still a mediator of God's continual voice in the world, reading it will fail to be revelatory or relevant to our spiritual quest. We must learn to read the Bible differently. The church must recover the reading of Scripture as a form of theological and spiritual devotion if it hopes to narrate its moral and practical life together. "All Scripture is inspired by God and is useful to teach us what is true and to make us realize what is wrong in our lives. It corrects us when we are wrong and teaches us to do what is right."[9]

This is not to say that understanding is easy or without complexity. But it does mean that God has made enough known to us in Scripture for us to live our lives in faithful devotion, producing a life of substance. To disregard the Bible as a myth or as irrelevant to our daily lives is to simply accept another myth, another narrative or script with which to live life.

Some "work," written or unwritten, *will* script our lives. For some it is the "success" script: your worth is defined by how successful you are. Others believe in the "intellectual" script: to be important and significant is to have acquired knowledge and academic degrees. Still others hold to the "beauty" script: staying fit and good-looking is life's highest goal.

What I'm suggesting here is that, for those who claim the name of Jesus, it may be a good thing to allow the Word of God to dwell deeply enough in your heart that you may be conscious of what is ultimately scripting your life. Everyone lives under what is called a "metanarrative," whether they like it or not. If success is your script, you will disdain and hate those who are unsuccessful. If beauty is your script, you will look down on or feel pity for those you judge as ugly.

Americans hold on tightly to the individualism script. "Anything that would violate our right to think for ourselves, judge for ourselves, make our own decisions, live our lives as we see fit, is not only morally wrong, it is sacrilegious."[10] Individualism is the script enacted every day in the lives of millions. This script is dangerous in that if we take it to the extreme, we may lose touch with the joy of dependence and the intimacy of community. For those who live their lives as individuals determined to express their freedom in any way they can, they may be in the long run "condemned to freedom."[11]

Alasdair MacIntyre adds compelling insights to this part of the American script:

> Contemporary moral experience as a consequence has a paradoxical character. For each of us is taught to see himself or herself as an autonomous moral agent; but each of us also becomes engaged by modes of practice, aesthetic or bureaucratic, which involve us in manipulative relationships with others. Seeking to protect the autonomy that we have learned to prize, we aspire ourselves not to be manipulated by others.[12]

In other words, we are so convinced of our autonomy and the script of individualism that our moral choices are easily manipulated in favor of our selves. Selfishness becomes our highest virtue.

Ponder for a moment your deepest hates and your greatest loves. It is these things that will reveal to you the type of script you're building your life around.

Even though so-called postmodern theory rejects unifying or totalizing modes of theory as rationalist myths of the enlightenment, every person still, whether they like it or not, lives under a "theory" or script that gives them a sense of how the world works, even if that script is the belief that there is no such thing as a script.[13] As humble as we like to think we are, most of us cannot escape believing that our way of life is the best way of life.

As Christians, we must attempt to live our lives in light of God's truth, and therefore must think deeply about the powers that are narrating our lives. "The Christian story, though it is but one tradition among others, necessarily makes a number of universal claims and cannot avoid the fact that it offers the world a 'metanarrative.'"[14] Many of us may be like John Nash, living in a false story guided by a faulty script. Recovering the Bible helps us purify our vision of the world and our lives, and can guide the way in scripting our spirituality.

Scripting Our Spirituality

I was a child actor. It was less exciting than it sounds. Living not far from Hollywood, my mother thought it a good idea to get her children involved in the entertainment industry at a young age. We all were show-offs, so it was a reasonable way to channel our energy. I had an agent, went on auditions, performed in plays and short films, and spent hours on sets. One of the disciplines I learned from this early exposure to acting was the ability to memorize large portions of text. In preparation for important auditions, I would be given a large portion of the script by my agent. Sometimes the script was for a comedy, and therefore I would practice my comedic delivery and timing. Other times it was for a drama, for which I would spend hours trying to cry on cue. The script determined my action. If I embodied the script, I would secure the job. I did not invent or write the script, I just received it and attempted to perform it as best as I could. The script I was handed shaped my performance.

Is it conceivable that Shakespeare was being more than poetic when he penned, "All the world's a stage, and all the men and women merely players"? From the moment we are born, we are handed scripts that hold our interest. We are actors in a great cosmic play and yet are often unaware of how this shapes who we are and how we live life.

In his book *A Mandate to Difference*, Walter Brueggemann explores the role that scripts play in forming us.[15] He believes that for Americans there are predominant scripts that make us who we are. The foremost scripts of both individuals and groups in our culture are therapy, technology, consumerism, and militarism.[16]

According to Brueggemann, we are handed a therapeutic script that tells us we are supposed to feel good, which includes working hard to retain youthfulness. In addition we are offered a technological script that assures us every problem we face will have a technological fix for it. The script of consumerism propels us to believe that a fulfilling life is marked by the accumulation of goods, whereas the militarism script positions America as uniquely exceptional, and her God-ordained prosperity needs to be retained whatever the cost. These are but a few examples of the influential scripts we are given in this culture.

⸻

As noted earlier, the question is not whether we are following a script in living our lives but rather if we are following a script that is in line with the author of life himself, Jesus Christ. To be a follower of Jesus is to be a person who is utterly convinced that the life he lived on earth and the life he invites us to partake in is the healthiest way of scripting our spirituality. Thus Scripture must retain its prominence in the lives of individual Christians as well as the church collectively if we are going to rightly narrate our relationship with God.

> We read Scripture in order to be refreshed in our memory and understanding of the story within which we ourselves are actors, to be reminded where it has come from and where it is going to, and hence what our own part within it ought to be.[17]

For the church to truly capture and perform the power of our witness, our approach to Scripture must have the goal of not merely acquiring biblical knowledge but rather cultivating the biblical drama in our very lives together. This requires that we become readers of the Scripture within communities again. For too long Christians in America have read the Bible as a form of personal piety. This is not a bad thing in itself, but there are liabilities with reading this way. Among them is the sense that Scripture reading is solely a personal and private spiritual discipline that further inculcates the believer to a private faith.

But our reading of the Scripture is not intended to be a one-person play. We are called to be disciplined readers of Scripture so that we can become lively performers of it. The church, in this way, is a drama troupe called by God to dramatically demonstrate the epic, sweeping story of Scripture in local communities.

The Bible is a tool to infuse God's people with the sacred memory of God's dealings with his people throughout the ages in the hopes of liberating us from the trivial scripts given to us throughout our lives. Trivial pursuits are simply the outgrowth of following a false script. The Bible confronts our triviality and offers a counter-narrative intended to guide us to the truth, and "then you will know the truth, and the truth will set you free."[18]

Though we are called to love and live by the Bible, we mustn't worship it. The author, not the script, deserves our ultimate adoration. Or, as N. T. Wright says, "The Bible is not an end in itself. It is there so that, by its proper use, the creator may be glorified and the creation may be healed. It is our task to be the people through whom this extraordinary vision comes to pass."[19]

Bringing the Scriptures back into our communal life together will no doubt empower followers of Jesus with the ability to discern where God is and what his will is in a world such as ours. The Scripture is a "light to our path" that will guide us home in an increasingly foggy and treacherous world. Through the Scriptures we will begin to live in rhythm with God once again.

The Scriptures attune our lives and hearts to God's. The Scriptures ultimately teach us that Jesus is the restorative power of God's love. He is our example of a "living text," the Word of God become flesh. Jesus came to this earth to die for our sins and redeem us, of course, but there's more to the story than that. He came to live the life that you and I didn't live; he came to live in rhythm with God and to enact the scriptural story from start to finish. And so, if the world has lost its script, the church, the body of Christ, must recover God's sacred play and become method actors on a chaotic stage.

Questions for Reflection

Why do so many people confess belief in the Bible but know so little of its content?

What role does the Bible play in your life? How does it shape your life story?

Do you agree that most people live as actors to a script? If so, what scripts do you think most shape the lives of people you know? If not, what stories, if any, help people make sense out of their lives?

What would it look like for the church to perform the Scriptures in their cities? How would church practices look different than they do today?

11

Transforming the Trivial

The power and influence of Rome was—and still is—without historical peer. The peace of Rome, the *pax romana*, covered, or more rightly conquered, vast stretches of the globe. With its rule came language, power, art, religion, culture, and politics. Small tribes and nations were brought under the reign of Roman Imperial power, creating unity among diversity. The reign of Rome was thought to be eternal. No one could have ever imagined that this "city on a hill" would become a laid-low ghetto. But all good things, even empires, come to an end. Civilizations do not come with a lifetime warranty. This was certainly true of Rome.

Most scholars agree that sometime in September 476, the final Roman emperor, Romulus Augustus, was overthrown by a Germanic prince named Odovacar, who with his hoards of warriors had gained domination of the leftovers of the Roman army. The Roman Empire had occupied much of what we now know as Western Europe for five hundred years, yet within only a small period of time its single emperor was replaced by dozens of kings and princes. But the decline of Rome did not take place in a day.

A great civilization is not conquered from without until it has destroyed itself within. The essential cause of Rome's decline lay in her people, her morals, her class struggle, her failing trade, her bureaucratic despotism, her stifling taxes, her consuming wars.[1]

It was a slow cancer in the womb of Rome herself that took the life of this great empire. Imagine what it would have been like if you were an average citizen of the Roman Empire in the aftermath of its fall. The very culture that was the backdrop of your life was swept away. With the death of Rome, Western Europe was ushered into what is referred to as the "dark ages," a time when unity was exchanged for confusion and when the world was splintered into thousands of tribes and factions all clamoring for survival in the eclipse of the eternal city. With the loss of Rome came the loss of civility. The moral consciousness of the people was in disarray. Society eroded and was in desperate need of cultivation.

Could we be living in or rapidly approaching a new "dark ages"? Could our confusion about what is good—or even if there is good—and who is good be a sign that we have suffered a loss of script? Does our current time mirror the decline and ultimate death of Rome from years past?

Alasdair MacIntyre believes so. In his acclaimed book *After Virtue*, he chronicles the loss of moral language, civility, and the practice of virtue in the Western world, drawing a parallel between the decline of Rome and our day. His words are so profound that I dare to quote him in length:

> If my account of our moral condition is correct [one characterized by moral incoherence and unsettleable moral disputes in the modern world], we ought to conclude that for some time now we too have reached that turning point. What matters at this stage is the construction of local forms of community within which civility and the intellectual and moral life can be sustained through the new dark ages which are already upon us. And if the tradition of the virtues was able

to survive the horrors of the last dark ages, we are not entirely without grounds for hope. This time however the barbarians are not waiting beyond the frontiers; they have already been governing us for quite some time. And it is our lack of consciousness of this that constitutes part of our predicament. We are waiting not for a Godot, but for another—doubtless very different—St. Benedict.[2]

I want to draw our attention to one specific passage in this text, namely, "What matters at this stage is the construction of local forms of community within which civility and the intellectual and moral life can be sustained through the new dark ages which are already upon us." MacIntyre shares an astonishing truth here that we should give great attention. In a world in disarray, the only solution for recovering the life of the mind and spirit is local communities that practice a special way of being in the world. He uses Saint Benedict as the example of this.

Saint Benedict is accredited for helping to bring Western Europe out of the dark ages through the establishment of monasteries all over the vast landscapes of the former Roman Empire. These monasteries were centers of learning and culture, of agriculture and sustainable living, as well as being home to spiritual renewal in the newly re-formed world. These "local forms of community" became the womb that would birth the medieval world. There would never have been a Thomas Aquinas if there had not first been a Saint Benedict. His mission played a large role in creating a new world of learning, progress, and human innovation. And it all started in a monastery.

━ ━ ━ ━

Our society has, in my view, exchanged depth for shallowness at a scale that is sure to have alarming implications. Our trivial pursuits are expressions of people living in a world where the eternal city has perished. That eternal city is the place of God in our midst. We have inherited and practiced a way of life in Western society that has marginalized the order God brings, and we have settled for the scraps of pleasure and knowledge left over. Whether we place our hope in money, success, or looking young; or cheapen our quest for knowledge; or even desire to conquer death; it seems to me that our passions are less guided by clarity and truth, and appear to be like the starving wanderings of a ravenous wolf rather than mimicking the penetrating precision of a heat-seeking missile.

In other words, welcome to the new dark ages.

The church must recover what it means to be witnesses of an altogether different reality than the world has to offer and relearn how to embody a form of life that engenders curiosity and allure. The church can be the one place where people reject illusions for reality and thus experience life in its full abundance. The church needs to take on a missional role in our world as a humble and effective culture-making community. The purpose of the church is not to escape culture, but to saturate it with transcendent beauty that can't be bought or sold or morphed into a holographic image. The goal of the church is to be a sacred community of cultural creation rather than a place of cultural capitulation.

Church and Culture

What do people believe is the role of the church in response to culture? For some, the church must be an isolated community that preserves a certain way of life unblemished from the wider society. I would call this the church in "retreat" mode. The Amish come to mind here. The wider culture is sick and polluted, and the only way people can keep themselves clean is by retreating into conclaves of sanctified safe houses called the church. This is a very sterile way of being Christian, not to mention that it leads to legalism. The "us versus them" mentality thrives in such a retreat mode. Though I think culture is not neutral, the idea of escaping it is absurd. We are it and it is us. The only question is who holds the keys.

In stark contrast to the retreat mode is what I call the "replicate" mode. This is an "If you can't beat 'em, join 'em" mentality. Protestant liberalism, for instance, would be an example of this strategy of being church. Culture is driving the church rather than the other way around. The church in this mode is almost constantly apologizing for being the church, promising the culture that it is progressing toward relevance. The only problem is, a church that is totally relevant to the culture is a church that is so blended in with the culture that it makes itself of little use.

I want to suggest that the mode the church should take is that of "renovation." Christians are in the recycling business. We take what was created for good and broken for bad and renovate it for new use. The church is called by God to be in the world but not of it. In doing so the church is worldlier than the world—an irony for certain—because it is made up of people who trust that the world is a gift given by God rather than a mistake left for human exploitation. The reasons Christians care about the environment, justice, human rights, physical and mental health, the life of the mind and spirit, and the deepening of all human experience is because they are aware of the astonishing gift of life and are determined to constantly offer thanks to its giver. To trivialize or pervert the gift in any way is to smack the face of God. The church is invited to be the light of the world within the darkest of ages. To do this it must be salt and leaven in culture. Practically, how can the church do this? I think we need to become clowns and curators.

Foolish Clowns

In medieval times jesters, what we would call clowns, were hired by kings and queens to entertain guests at large banquets. They would juggle, perform tricks, and make fun of guests at the party. They were the standup comedians of the ancient world. One of the interesting abilities of a jester was to take that which was taboo or held in high esteem and make fun of it. The king, for instance, was so powerful that no one would dare to tease him or ridicule him. To do so would certainly mean imminent and violent death. Yet jesters, dressed to look like buffoons, were given a special standing in the royal courts. Many jesters would, like comedians of our day, make hilarious fun of the royalty attending the party. The king's pomp would be imitated, gestures mimicked, and even physical attributes exploited for the entertainment of guests. Under no other circumstance could the weaknesses or ugly attributes of royalty be made fun of, but it just so happened that a jester dressed in mask and makeup was able to bring to life the hidden thoughts and feelings of the masses.

The jester was a clown who revealed the folly of royalty. No doubt many in attendance at the banquet shared the same sentiments as the jester, but because they were not wearing the correct clothing, their views would be seen as condemning and offensive. Watching the jester do what they could not do and say what they could not say must have given a sort of cathartic feeling to those in attendance. Laughter brought relief. The jester was able to, in subtle and humorous ways, unmask the king's power and show him for who he really was, namely a man just like everyone else, inching his way toward eternity.

We live in a world of very powerful kings. Money, entertainment, celebrity, media, and power are all "kings" seated on our cultural throne. I'd like to suggest that the church must play the role of a clown in a culture of king worship. What do I mean?

I truly believe those who invest their lives in trivial things starve their souls and do not satisfy their longings. The human soul was created by God, and in the words of Augustine "is restless until it finds rest in you, oh God."[3] The only problem is in our world God has been swept away from the horizon, so we are left with lesser idols to try to satiate our desperation.

The idols of this world can and do fill us, for a short while, but they cannot meet our deepest need. Perhaps the reason the world is consumed with triviality is because we lack living examples of people who show the kings for what they are, who unmask the powers of our culture as temporal and expose them as cheap answers to eternal questions.

Remember Paul calls the gospel "foolishness."[4] Our goal should be to say publicly what many believe, deep down, privately. In other words, we should show that money is just money, youth is just youth, beauty is just beauty, and entertainment is just entertainment. Using "just" as a way to describe the trivial is more than appropriate. Like the jester who was able to taunt the king by not taking him seriously, the church ought to recover practices that exploit the emptiness of our cultural idols.

Again, we are not called to retreat or replicate but to renovate. The problem with many of us is that we worship the kings of our world and in doing so neglect the true King of the Universe. When we encounter God we are able to demystify the cultural icons of our day, while at the same time appreciate them for what they truly are, because we ultimately refuse to make them what they are not—namely the king of our hearts.

The church has always been called to expose what is believed to be powerful as weak and proclaim that which is thought to be weak as powerful. This is the extraordinary irony of our faith. The only way we can be of any help in our culture is by living within it as agents of renovation. This action is fueled by the belief that we can expose the myths of our time, not only for their demise but also for their redemption. I agree with Walter Wink when he writes, "I believe that even these rebellious Powers can be transformed in the crucible of God's Love."[5]

What role can the church play in assisting in such a transformation? In addition to being clowns, we must also become curators of beauty, grace, and hope.

Curators of Beauty

What is a curator? The word comes from the Latin *curare*, which means "to take care." A curator is an overseer or keeper of a certain cultural heritage. Most familiar to us today is an art gallery or museum curator who "takes care" of the selection of art or artifacts on display in their various exhibits. Their job is to make sure there is a consistent expression of life and beauty on display in their venue. To be a good curator you need to be both in touch with the history of the art as well as the needs of those who will view your selections. This embodies a delicate balance between a devotion to the art form and the needs of the viewer. The church must once again become curators of culture.

We must remember that the church commissioned the greatest art in history. Symphonies and requiems, murals and tapestries, the life of the mind as well as the cultivation of beauty were projects the church held in high esteem. We have lost this and have settled for replicating cultural fads instead. But beauty is part of our mission.

If we are going to transform culture, we must regain our position in the world as a curator of beauty. This means that instead of retreating from media, we must renovate it, exposing what needs rehabilitation and remolding it for good. It is the responsibility of every church to enliven their congregation to infuse life into every sphere of culture. We are to be clowns who refuse to worship the kings of culture, as well as curators who outdo and ultimately inspire our cultural cohabitants. The church ought to be at the forefront of sponsoring the arts as a means of having a stake in the cultural battles of our time.

As those who worship the Creator, we are endowed with a "sneak peek" into the heart of God, which must be expressed through beauty in all its forms. Films, plays, sculpture, and music should spill out the doors of the church and into the world. If this was a serious priority of the church, we would be able to shuck the skin of copying culture and begin creating culture. If we do not do this, we will be left with copying culture as the only way to retain relevance. And in the end we will never engage or change culture but will merely mimic it.

We must heed the words of Andy Crouch when he writes,

> The greatest danger of copying culture, as a posture, is that it may well become all too successful. We end up creating an entire subcultural world within which Christians comfortably move and have their being without ever encountering the broader cultural world they are imitating. We breed a generation that prefers facsimile to reality, simplicity to complexity (for cultural copying, almost by definition, ends up sanding off the rough and surprising edges of any cultural good it appropriates), and familiarity to novelty. Not only is this a generation incapable of genuine creative participation in the ongoing drama of human culture making, it is dangerously detached from a God who is anything but predictable and safe.[6]

I could not agree more with Crouch's assessment, and thus use his warning as a charge to the church to become invested in culture as curators of beauty.

Curators of Grace

The church has one, and only one, message to offer the world that it cannot by its own power offer itself: namely, the message of grace. "For the law was given through Moses; grace and truth came through Jesus Christ."[7]

The apostle Paul begins all his letters with the words "grace and peace." Grace, in the words of Paul Tillich, is "the courage to accept acceptance."[8] It is a free offer of love to a busy and hardened heart. Grace sees beauty in age, wealth in gray hair, rising stock values in a story of faith. Grace is the only antidote to a world of trivial pursuits. Why so? Because it is our lack of grace that pushes our insatiable wants onward. It is our deep feeling of inadequacy, of not measuring up, that manipulates our passions to strive toward a vast mirage of perishing promises. It is our deep feelings of shame, judgment, self-hatred, fear, and isolation that fuel our entertainment-obsessed, money-driven, death-defying, instant-gratification culture.

The gods we end up worshiping are very unforgiving. Money cannot express grace to the poor; beauty will not offer grace to the ugly; entertainment cannot give grace to the satisfied; medicine cannot give grace to the dying. False gods only take, they never give. Only the God found and expressed in Jesus Christ is powerful enough to give us the strength to believe in and receive grace, and thus end our trivial preoccupations.

Grace is the tool that will chisel free even the hardest of hearts. Therefore the church must, and I mean *must*, become curators of grace in our communities. The oppressed, the misused, the victimized, the forgotten, the poor who are rich, and the rich who are poor, the beautiful and deformed—Jesus's followers must take care to see that grace is being freely distributed to everyone, never running out of our supply. We do so not from a position of superiority, but as those who have also been freed of our trivial idols and are determined to seek God for continued favor and help.

Tim Keller writes,

> We think we've learned about grace, set our idols aside, reached a place where we're serving God not for what we're going to get from him but for who he is. There's a certain sense in which we spend our entire lives thinking we've reached the bottom of our hearts and finding it is a false bottom. Mature Christians are not people who have completely hit the bedrock. I do not believe that is possible in this life. Rather, they are people who know how to keep drilling and are getting closer and closer.[9]

The church must take care to keep on digging, so as to get closer to and more accustomed to grace.

Curators of Hope

The opening chapter of the book of Genesis is telling. The Scriptures teach that in the beginning there was nothing, absolutely nothing. Darkness covered the emptiness of a world yet to be born. This world was chaotic and empty, lacking in form and substance. In a moment of powerful inventiveness the Triune God, the God who is all power, beauty, majesty, love, goodness, joy, happiness, and hope, spoke into the nothingness. Our God is the God of substance, not emptiness. Our God is the God of light, not darkness. Our God is the God of creation, not destruction. So God looked over the darkness, the chaotic empty mess of a world yet to be born, and by the power of his Word, by the power of his language and his speech, God began to speak in poetic written form, demanding that the emptiness and darkness be transformed.

"Let there be light," God commands, and there was light, and God pronounced the light to be good. The first burst of light was the beginning of hope for a chaotic world. God continued to create plant life and animals and the sun and moon, calling them all good. In creating human beings God announced over them their sacred dignity; they are "very good," made in the very image of the Creator. Like the Creator they are to cultivate and create.

Unfortunately the story of sin is that we choose destruction over creation. That choice still happens on every street corner, in every heart and home, in the lives of all of us. Yet as bad as the world may be, God has not stopped creating and breathing new life into it. God is still a curator of hope.

In Ephesians 2:10, Paul writes of those redeemed by Jesus, saying, "We are God's handiwork, created in Christ Jesus to do good works." Several words demand our attention in this verse. The first word is *handiwork*, the second word is *creative*, and the third word is *good*.

The word *handiwork* in the Greek language is *poiema*. It is the word from which we get our word *poem*. Paul says that we are God's poem created to do good works, just as God did when he created the world. In other words, we are agents of hope, commissioned by God to be part of the renovation of the world. You are a curator of hope.

If we know one thing for certain, it is that trivial pursuits cannot ultimately give hope. When people are left empty and dry from pursuing empty promises, the church can—we can—be a curator of hope pointing the way to God among the ashes. God created us; none of us is an accident. God created us to live in poetic rhythm with him. God takes our lives and shines in us with his rhythmic love, reminding us who we truly are and commissioning us to be curators of hope. In a world that worships beauty, power, money, and strength, the weakest and frailest among us who exhibit hope may be the most powerful prophets of our time.

━━━ ━━━

Loren is a dear friend of mine. He leads one of the most significant, richest lives of anyone I've ever met. Loren was born with cerebral palsy, but he's an exuberant, God-bathed human being. Loren is the opposite of what our trivial culture aspires to be. He's blind in one eye, crippled in one hand, has difficulty generating income, and is uninterested in pop culture fads or celebrity worship. Inside Loren's frail frame lives a power that no corporate CEO or celebrity can compete with. Inspired by, and honestly just as confused by, his powerful outlook on life, I took my friend out to lunch one time to discover his secret.

As we were eating our messy burgers and fries, I looked long into the shining but scarred face of my friend. Beside us were a table of beautiful girls discussing a fashion magazine. On the television fastened to the wall flickered news of the volatile stock market. Overwhelmed by his spirit, and in some way jealous of his spiritual fervor, I dared to ask Loren a question I had wondered for years.

"Loren, do you ever get mad at God for your situation? I mean do you ever ask in anger, 'Why me?'"

I began to ponder all that Loren would not experience because of his condition. He would never drive a car, and most likely would never get married or have kids; many things that most of us take for granted are fantasies to him.

"Are you ever so angry with God, that you disbelieve in his goodness?" I added. "Do you ever lose hope?"

I waited patiently for his response. Slowly Loren put down his large burger, looked deep into my eyes, and said, "No, I never do." A big smile came to his face.

I don't know what I expected him to say, but this simple, sincere response was shocking to me.

"Ian, you know, God uses me," he said. "He especially uses my brokenness. It gives people hope, I think."

I then remembered the life Loren lived. He served in ministries working with people more handicapped than he, served the homeless on Tuesdays, and stuffed bulletins on Sundays. He was a secret agent in God's kingdom.

Then he said something so profound that it has marked me to this day. He began to describe the depths of God's love for him. He spoke of Jesus as the giver of life, the forgiver, the healer, and ultimately the giver of hope. Though my friend Loren was kept from enjoying the "good things" of life, whatever that may mean, he was freed by his weakness to enjoy God as his greatest treasure.

Then he began to speak about the hope he had in Jesus. He trusted that Jesus would one day make his crooked body straight, his blind eye see, and his feeble legs dance. "I live my life by hope, Ian," he said, "not much else." Then he concluded with a statement that brought tears to my eyes: "How can I be angry at a God like that?"

I looked at my friend Loren, and I said with excitement, "What you have told me, Loren, is the gospel, that's the good news if I've ever heard it!"

But he quickly replied, "No, it's not."

Now at that time I was a sophomore biblical studies undergraduate, which meant I knew enough to be annoying and a danger to myself and others. I was about to pontificate to my friend Loren the real meaning of the word *gospel*. That, in Greek, it in fact does mean "good news." But before the words could leave my lips, before I could preach an exegetical sermon, Loren looked at me and said, "Ian, it's not good news, it's *great* news."

The world longs for great news, doesn't it? If the church is to be a curator of hope, we must remember that our task is to live, breathe, speak, and perform the "great news" of the gospel wherever God places us. It is our sovereign responsibility to be curators of hope in a world of despair. No act of man, no scheme of humankind can offer us a cure for hopelessness. Only God in Christ can do this. What would the church look like if its mission was to become a curator of hope? I would guess it would look a little like Loren: frail, broken, humble, available, and shining with a secret and with surprising power that burns like the sun no matter how dark the age. May we be a church like that. That is my hope and prayer. Amen!

Questions for Reflection

Think of a time when God transformed an area of your life. What feelings and words come to mind when you think of God's transformative presence in your life?

We spoke of different postures the church can take toward the world as retreat, replicate, and renovate. Which posture do you think is most practiced in churches, and why?

The apostle Paul refers to the gospel of the cross as foolishness. He means that God saves in ways that most people would think are silly at first glance. What are some practices Christians could do to show the foolish love of God in a world concerned with image?

We spoke of being cultural curators. What are some of your life ambitions? How could your gifts, passions, and abilities be used for the renovation of culture and the glory of God?

Conclusion

What Now?

A book is the result of a mind unwinding itself on paper. Here I offer a humble wink to readers who have attended to my unwinding thus far.

I have attempted to evaluate certain popular cultural phenomena with an eye toward whether they offer us deeper avenues of self-discovery or are merely time-occupying diversions from life's most pressing questions. My hope was not only to cast a critical eye but also, through observation, raise suspicion in our minds about many of our assumed and unevaluated habits that shape much of who we are. My goal in making these observations is to expose the shallowness of much of our contemporary obsessions for the purpose of forcing us to confront whether or not our search for meaning is slipping away in the wake of trivial pursuits. This criticism is meant, ultimately, to be constructive.

My true intention is to begin a conversation about what it would look like if the church could become a sacred island in the world, an island where meaning and depth and beauty are cultivated in excess and which, in turn, becomes a cultural force to be reckoned with. And my hope is that this book sparks the beginnings of two changes.

First, a heightened sense of *observation*. If people start to become more attuned to what forces form their thinking and action, I would be deeply satisfied. I want this book to create some space, some breathing room to allow us to reflect on the world from a different perspective so that we can see the world in a different way. My prayer is that this space would allow us to evaluate how we spend our time and energies—and, most of all, how what occupies us may be either harming or helping our image as beloved children of God. If people start observing more rather than allowing life and cultural fads to just wash over them, I believe I have done a bit of what I set out to do.

Second, greater and more purposeful *engagement*. My ultimate hope is that people would begin to engage more in the life of the mind and heart. The complexity of the world is overwhelming and, as noted, causes many to fall out of the fight to know themselves. If I could snap my fingers to engender one response, it would be that we all write down lists of perplexing questions or audacious goals of both soul and mind, and would not rest until answers and experience come. The world needs fully engaged and alive people who search after truth, know his name, and proclaim him to the world. This means that we, as Christians, have the responsibility to engage in the world not as passive spectators but as fully engaged members who share a desire for the common good. In our engagement we must not lose sight of why we engage and who for. Personally and publicly, it would benefit the world if Christians were models of souls made alive by the glory of God who spark life wherever they go.

Finally, for those who are leaders in the church, I write this as a brother who stands in solidarity with you and your church. I believe our "what now" is to stand courageously against the cultural tides that demean the gospel and weaken discipleship. As leaders we are given the charge to lead and shepherd God's family, and we will be judged more harshly because of our acceptance of the call. My prayer is that God would give each of us courage to preach the glorious good news of God in season and out. I pray that we would have the audacity to confront cultural idols who compete for the hearts of people or harm the spiritual lives of many. Mostly I pray and hope that we trust in God's ability to make our churches the most attractive, lively, and significant gatherings in our cities. This is not because we have state-of-the-art sound and video equipment but because God is there and that is enough. I would encourage us all to make our leadership decisions with God's ultimate end in mind. If God's vision is to have the world worship him alone, turning from idols and lesser gods, then in our thoughts and actions we must work toward that end. We must not do so through negative criticisms of the world but rather through creating a better world. Beauty is more persuasive than anger. Help the world see how beautiful Jesus is and the rest will take care of itself.

My prayer for all is that Jesus would become more present to us, alive and vibrant, tearing apart our illusions so as to give us a new vision. My prayer is that the substance of God and the story of his love for the world will spark divine innovation in each of us, making us actors in his divine play, curators of his beauty, and clowns smiling at the absurd greatness of his love.

Amen.

Notes

Introduction

1. Proverbs 18:15.

Chapter 1 The Self under Siege

1. "Generation M2: Media in the Lives of 8- to 18-Year-Olds," Henry J. Kaiser Family Foundation, January 1, 2010, http://www.kff.org/entmedia/8010.cfm.

2. "Oscar Wilde," *Encyclopaedia Britannica*, accessed October 3, 2013, http://www.britannica.com/EBchecked/topic/643631/Oscar-Wilde/643631suppinfo/Supplemental-Information.

3. Archibald Hart, *Thrilled to Death: How the Endless Pursuit of Pleasure Is Leaving Us Numb* (Nashville: Thomas Nelson, 2007), 32.

4. Neil Postman, *Amusing Ourselves to Death: Public Discourse in the Age of Show Business* (New York: Penguin Books, 2005), 3.

5. Robert Putnam, *Bowling Alone: The Collapse and Revival of American Community* (New York: Simon & Schuster Paperbacks, 2000), 246.

6. Christian Smith, *Souls in Transition: The Religious and Spiritual Lives of Emerging Adults* (New York: Oxford Press, 2009), 168.

7. Ibid.

8. Ibid.

9. "W. B. Yeats Quotes," *Good Reads*, accessed October 3, 2013, http://www.goodreads.com/quotes/754152-it-takes-more-courage-to-examine-the-dark-corners-of.

10. Romans 1:25.

11. Jonathan Lear, *Radical Hope: Ethics in the Face of Cultural Devastation* (Massachusetts: Harvard University Press, 2006), 83.

12. 2 Timothy 3:1–5, emphasis added.

13. Chris Hedges, *Empire of Illusion* (New York: Nation Books, 2009), 27.

14. Augustine, *The City of God*, trans. by Marcus Dods (Peabody, MA: Hendrickson Publishers, 2008), 410.

Chapter 2 The Light of the World

1. United States Department of Labor, Bureau of Labor Statistics, "American Time Use Survey Summary," economic news release, June 22, 2012, http://www.bls.gov/news.release/atus.nr0.htm.

2. Hedges, *Empire of Illusion*, 44.

3. Mark Poster, ed., *Jean Baudrillard: Selected Writings* (Cambridge: Stanford University Press, 2001), 40.

4. Craig Detweiler and Barry Taylor, *A Matrix of Meanings: Finding God in Pop Culture* (Grand Rapids: Baker Academic, 2003), 191.

5. Putnam, *Bowling Alone*, 240.

6. Detweiler and Taylor, *A Matrix of Meanings*, 192.

7. Ibid., 191.

8. Slavoj Zizek, "Will You Laugh for Me, Please," accessed August 29, 2013, http://www.lacan.com/zizeklaugh.htm.

9. Ibid.

10. Andy Warhol, *Moderna Museet Exhibition Catalogue*, Stockholm, February 1968.

11. "I Want a Famous Face," MTV.com, accessed August 29, 2013, http://www.mtv.com/shows/i_want_a_famous_face-2/series.jhtml.

12. Gordon Lynch, *Understanding Theology and Popular Culture* (Malden, MA: Blackwell Publishing, 2005), 54.

13. Ibid.

Chapter 3 I Bought My Soul on eBay

1. Associated Press, "eBay Blocks Man's Attempt to Sell Soul," *USA Today*, February 6, 2002, http://www.usatoday.com/tech/news/2001-02-09-ebay-soul.htm.

2. "Man Auctions Ad Space on Forehead," *BBC News*, January 10, 2005, http://news.bbc.co.uk/i/hi/technology/416413.stm.

3. William Cavanaugh, *Being Consumed: Economics and Christian Desire* (Grand Rapids: Eerdmans, 2008), 33.

4. Ibid.

5. Joshua Rhett Miller, "Arkansas Mother Sells Naming Rights of Unborn Son on eBay," *Fox News*, August 5, 2009, http://www.foxnews.com/story/2009/08/05/arkansas-mother-sells-naming-rights-unborn-son-on-ebay/.

6. Ethan Trex, "Dogs, Ferrari, Strangers—Weird Stipulations," August 31, 2009, http://www.cnn.com/2009/LIVING/wayoflife/08/31/bizarre.will.stipulations/index.html.

7. James Truslow Adams, *The Epic of America* (Piscataway, NJ: Transaction Publishers, 2012), 308.

8. Robert Bellah, Richard Madsen, William Sullivan, Ann Swidler, and Steven M. Tipton, *Habits of the Heart: Individualism and Commitment in American Life* (Los Angeles: University of California Press, 1996), 142.

9. Blanche Evans, "New Homes: Will the Big Home Downsize?," *Realty Times*, June 19, 2006, http://realtytimes.com/rtpages/20060619_downsizinghomes.htm.

10. Matthew 6:31–33 ESV.

11. Amanda Smith interview with Alain de Botton, "Status Anxiety," *Book Talk*, May 29, 2004, http://www.abc.net.au/radionational/programs/booktalk/status-anxiety/3627572#transcript.

12. Ibid.

13. This phrase made famous by Art Buchwald.

14. 1 Corinthians 6:19–20.

15. Dietrich Bonhoeffer, *Ethics* (Minneapolis: Fortress Press, 2009), 82.

16. 1 Timothy 6:10.

Chapter 4 Google Stole My Brain

1. Debbie Lee Wesselmann, *Trutor and the Balloonist* (San Francisco: Mac-Adam/Cage Publishing, 1997), 199.

2. As a nonscientist, I venture to explain this peculiar feature of the human makeup only by encouraging the reader to look up such concepts in depth.

3. Joseph Hardy and Michael Scanlon, "The Science Behind Lumosity," November 2009, http://www.lumosity.com/documents/the_science_behind_lumosity.pdf.

4. Joseph Hardy, "High Level of Evidence for Cognitive Training," June 7, 2010, http://www.lumosity.com/blog/high-level-of-evidence-for-cognitive-training/.

5. "Lumosity.com – Why I Play – Retiring," YouTube video, 0:36, posted by Lumosity on July 18, 2013, http://www.youtube.com/watch?v=d3h_VOYcomg.

6. See Romans 12:2.

7. Nicholas Carr, *The Shallows: What the Internet Is Doing to Our Brains* (New York: W.W. Norton & Company, 2011), 192.

8. Nicholas Carr, "Is Google Making Us Stupid?," *Atlantic*, July 1, 2008, http://www.theatlantic.com/magazine/archive/2008/07/is-google-making-us-stupid/306868/.

9. Carr, *Shallows*, 5.

10. David Shenk, *Data Smog: Surviving the Information Glut* (New York: Harper One, 1998), 31.

11. Ibid., 30.

12. Roger E. Bohn and James E. Short, "How Much Information?: 2009 Report on American Consumers," Global Information Industry Center, University of California, San Diego, December 2009, http://hmi.ucsd.edu/pdf/HMI_2009_Consumer_Report_Dec9_2009.pdf.

13. See John 8:32.

14. Dallas Willard, *Hearing God: Developing a Conversational Relationship with God* (Downers Grove, IL: InterVarsity Press, 1999), 283.

15. Mark A. Noll, *The Scandal of the Evangelical Mind* (Grand Rapids: Eerdmans, 1994), 3–4.

Chapter 5 What's Your Status?

1. Stephen Marche, "Is Facebook Making Us Lonely?," *Atlantic*, April 2, 2012, http://www.theatlantic.com/magazine/archive/2012/05/is-facebook-making-us-lonely/308930/.

2. Ibid.

3. Ibid.

4. Ibid.

5. Katherine Brooks, "Face 2 Face: A Documentary Film," *Kickstarter*, April 5, 2011, http://www.kickstarter.com/projects/KatherineBrooks/face-2-facebook-a-documentary-film.

6. "Katherine Brooks, Documentarist," *Daily Brink*, May 11, 2011, http://www.dailybrink.com/?p=1398.

7. Dr. Jim Taylor, "Is Facebook Creating a False Self in Your Children?," Examiner.com, October 15, 2012, http://www.examiner.com/article/is-facebook-creating-a-false-self-your-children.

8. Ibid.

9. Ibid.

Chapter 6 Holograms Don't Die

1. Tiffany Hsu, "Japanese Pop Star Hatsune Miku Takes the Stage—as a 3-D Hologram," *Los Angeles Times*, November 10, 2010, http://latimesblogs.latimes.com/technology/2010/11/japanese-pop-star-takes-the-stage-as-a-3-d-hologram.html.

2. Ibid.

3. "Hatsune Miku - World Is Mine ~ Project DIVA Live - eng subs," YouTube video, 2:54, uploaded by VocaloidLiveConcert, August 12, 2012, http://www.youtube.com/watch?v=O17f3lB7BFY.

4. "Woody Allen Quotes," *Good Reads*, accessed October 3, 2013, http://www.goodreads.com/author/quotes/10356.Woody_Allen.

5. Ernest Becker, *The Denial of Death* (New York: Free Press Paperbacks, 1997).

6. "Manifesto of Little Monsters—What Does it All Mean?" *GaGa's Little Monsters*, May 19, 2010, http://gagaslittlemonster.wordpress.com/2010/05/19/manifesto-of-little-monsters-what-does-it-all-mean/.

7. "Albert Camus Quotes," *Think Exist*, accessed October 3, 2013, http://thinkexist.com/quotation/men_must_live_and_create-live_to_the_point_of/260211.html.

8. "Philosophy through Literature: That's Jean Paul Sartre," *Existentialism*, accessed August 29, 2013, http://homepages.spa.umn.edu/~valdez/phil.html.

9. "Quotes," *John Paul Sartre*, accessed October 4, 2013, http://www.sartre.org/quotes.htm.

10. Jack Cafferty, "$10 Billion Spent on Cosmetic Procedures Despite Recession," *Cafferty File*, March 10, 2010, http://caffertyfile.blogs.cnn.com/2010/03/10/10-billion-spent-on-cosmetic-procedures-despite-recession/.

11. Elaine Graham, "Post/Human Conditions," *Theology and Sexuality: The Journal for the Study of Christianity and Sexuality* 10, no. 2 (March 2004): 10.

12. Tom Templeton, "Holding Back the Years," *The Observer*, September 15, 2007, http://www.guardian.co.uk/lifeandstyle/2007/sep/16/healthandwellbeing.genetics.

13. "Where Is Thy Sting? - Quote by Aubrey de Grey," *Longecity*, August 12, 2003, http://www.longecity.org/forum/topic/1559-where-is-thy-sting-quote-by-aubrey-de-grey/.

14. I am indebted to Stanley Hauerwas for this phrase.

15. Psalm 90:12.

16. 1 Peter 1:24.

17. Psalm 103:14 NLT.

18. "'You've Got to Find What You Love,' Jobs Says," *Stanford Report*, June 14, 2005, emphasis added, http://news.stanford.edu/news/2005/june15/jobs-061505.html.

19. 2 Corinthians 4:16–18, emphasis added.

20. Thomas Merton, *No Man Is an Island* (New York: Harcourt Brace Jovanovich, 1983), 262–63.

Chapter 7 Xeroxed Jesus

1. Proverbs 27:6 NLT.
2. Hannah Arendt, "Between Past and Future: Eight Exercises in Political Thought," *The Crisis in Culture* (New York: Viking Press, 1968), 207.
3. Dietrich Bonhoeffer, *The Cost of Discipleship* (New York: Touchstone, 1995), 11.
4. A. W. Tozer, *The Root of the Righteous* (Camp Hill, PA: Wingspread Publishers, 1955), 125. Tozer does not represent my thinking on every issue, but here he makes a strong point that I believe speaks across the theological spectrum.
5. See Bob Burns, Tasha D. Chapman, and Donald Guthrie, *Resilient Ministry: What Pastors Told Us About Surviving and Thriving* (Downers Grove, IL: InterVarsity Press, 2013).
6. Matthew 5:13.
7. Matthew 20:25 NLT.
8. Martin Luther King Jr. "Letter from Birmingham City Jail," April 16, 1963, http://www.thekingcenter.org/archive/document/letter-birmingham-city-jail-0#.
9. Matthew 6:10.
10. Henri Nouwen, *In the Name of Jesus: Reflections on Christian Leadership* (New York: Crossroads Publishing, 1993), 35.

Chapter 8 Exchanging the Sacred for the Profane

1. Mircea Eliade, *The Sacred and The Profane: The Nature of Religion*, trans. by Willard R. Trask (Orlando: Harcourt, 1987).
2. Sigmund Freud, *Reflections on War and Death*, trans. by A. A. Brill and B. Kutner (New York: Moffat, Yard & Co., 1918), 16.
3. Sigmund Freud, *New Introductory Lectures on Psychoanalysis* (New York: W.W. Norton & Co., 1965), 216.
4. Basit Bilal Koshul, *The Postmodern Significance of Max Weber's Legacy* (New York: Palgrave Macmillan, 2005), 11.
5. Charles Taylor, *A Secular Age* (Massachusetts: Harvard Press, 2007), 25.
6. William Cavanaugh, *The Myth of Religious Violence* (New York: Oxford Press, 2009), 57.
7. Ibid., 58.
8. Ibid.
9. Søren Kierkegaard, *Attack upon Christendom*, trans. by Walter Lowrie (Princeton: Princeton University Press, 1968), 127.
10. C. S. Lewis, *Mere Christianity* (New York: Harper One, 1952), 136.
11. Eliade, *Sacred and Profane*, 23.
12. "When a Man Ceases to Worship God," The American Chesterton Society Research Services, accessed October 4, 2013, http://www.chesterton.org/discover-chesterton/frequently-asked-questions/cease-to-worship/.
13. James A. Herrick, *The Making of the New Spirituality: The Eclipse of the Western Religious Tradition* (Downers Grove, IL: InterVarsity, 2003), 17.

Chapter 9 Bringing Sacred Back

1. See Genesis 3:19.
2. Genesis 1:31.
3. Thomas Merton, *No Man Is an Island* (New York: Harcourt, 1983).

Chapter 10 Bringing Scripture Back

1. Stephen Prothero, *Religious Literacy: What Every American Needs to Know and Doesn't* (New York: HarperCollins, 2008), 6.

2. Ibid.

3. Ibid., 29.

4. Ibid., 30.

5. 1 Corinthians 13:12 NLT.

6. Acts 9:1–9.

7. Karl Barth, *Church Dogmatics: The Doctrine of the Word of God*, vol. I.1 (New York: T & T Clark, 2010), 110.

8. Søren Kierkegaard, *Provocations: Spiritual Writings of Kierkegaard* (Maryknoll, NY: Orbis Books, 2003), 56.

9. 2 Timothy 3:16 NLT.

10. Robert Bellah, Richard Madsen, William Sullivan, Ann Swidler, and Steven M. Tipton, *Habits of the Heart: Individualism and Commitment in American Life* (Los Angeles: University of California Press, 1996), 142.

11. Stanley Hauerwas, *The Peaceable Kingdom* (Notre Dame: University of Notre Dame Press, 1983), 7.

12. Alasdair MacIntyre, *After Virtue*, 2nd ed. (Notre Dame: University of Notre Dame Press, 1984), 68.

13. Steven Best and Douglas Kellner, *Postmodern Theory* (New York: Guilford Press, 1991), 38.

14. Bryan P. Stone, *Evangelism after Christendom: The Theology and Practice of Christian Witness* (Grand Rapids: Brazos, 2007), 42.

15. Walter Brueggemann, *A Mandate to Difference: An Invitation to the Contemporary Church* (Louisville: Westminster John Knox, 2007).

16. Ibid., 63.

17. N. T. Wright, *Scripture and the Authority of God: How to Read the Bible Today* (New York: Harper One, 2005), 116.

18. John 8:32.

19. N. T. Wright, "How Can the Bible Be Authoritative?," *Vox Evangelica*, vol. 21 (1991): 7–32, http://ntwrightpage.com/Wright_Bible_Authoritative.htm.

Chapter 11 Transforming the Trivial

1. Will Durant, *Caesar and Christ: The Story of Civilization* (New York: Simon & Schuster, 1972), 665.

2. MacIntyre, *After Virtue*, 244–45.

3. Augustine, *Confessions*, trans. by Henry Chadwick (Oxford: Oxford University Press, 1991), 3.

4. See 1 Corinthians 1:18, 23; 2:14.

5. Walter Wink, *The Powers That Be: Theology for a New Millennium* (New York: Doubleday, 1999), 10.

6. Andy Crouch, *Culture Making* (Downers Grove, IL: InterVarsity, 2008), 94.

7. John 1:17.

8. Paul Tillich, *The Courage to Be* (New Haven: Yale University Press, 2000).

9. Tim Keller, *Counterfeit Gods: The Empty Promises of Money, Sex, and Power and the Only Hope That Matters* (New York: Dutton, 2009), 89.

Ian DiOrio (MDiv, Fuller Theological Seminary; DMin, Azusa Pacific University) became a Christian in his twenties after spending his younger life in the underground music scene in Los Angeles as a DJ. Ian has served as a teaching pastor at Eastside Christian Church, and currently writes and speaks from Southern California. He was recently featured by *Christian Standard Magazine* as one of the top 40 leaders under 40. He is thrilled to be the husband of Julia and the father of Semeia, Asha, and Zion.

Learn more at www.iandiorio.org.